GOSPEL F⊕UNDATIONS

A Wandering People

| VOL. 2 | EXODUS – JUDGES |

LifeWay Press® • Nashville, Tennessee

From the creators of *The Gospel Project*, Gospel Foundations is a six-volume resource that teaches the storyline of Scripture. It is comprehensive in scope yet concise enough to be completed in just one year. Each seven-session volume includes videos to help your group understand the way each text fits into the storyline of the Bible.

ISBN 978-1-5359-0359-2 • Item 005803633

Dewey decimal classification: 230
Subject headings: CHRISTIANITY / GOSPEL / SALVATION

EDITORIAL TEAM

Michael Kelley
Director, Groups Ministry

Brian Dembowczyk
Managing Editor

Joel Polk
Editorial Team Leader

Daniel Davis, Josh Hayes
Content Editors

Brian Daniel
Manager, Short-Term Discipleship

Darin Clark
Art Director

We believe that the Bible has God for its author; salvation for its end; and truth, without any mixture of error, for its matter and that all Scripture is totally true and trustworthy. To review LifeWay's doctrinal guideline, please visit lifeway.com/doctrinalguideline.

To order additional copies of this resource, write to LifeWay Resources Customer Service; One LifeWay Plaza; Nashville, TN 37234; fax 615-251-5933; call toll free 800-458-2772; order online at LifeWay.com; email orderentry@lifeway.com; or visit the LifeWay Christian Store serving you.

Printed in the United States of America

Groups Ministry Publishing
LifeWay Resources
One LifeWay Plaza
Nashville, TN 37234

Contents

About *The Gospel Project*

Gospel Foundations is from the creators of *The Gospel Project*, which exists to point kids, students, and adults to the gospel of Jesus Christ through weekly group Bible studies and additional resources that show how God's plan of redemption unfolds throughout Scripture and still today, compelling them to join the mission of God.

The Gospel Project provides theological yet practical, age-appropriate Bible studies that immerse your entire church in the story of the gospel, helping to develop a gospel culture that leads to gospel mission.

Gospel Story

Immersing people of all ages in the storyline of Scripture: God's plan to rescue and redeem His creation through His Son, Jesus Christ.

Gospel Culture

Inspiring communities where the gospel saturates our experience and doubters become believers who become declarers of the gospel.

Gospel Mission

Empowering believers to live on mission, declaring the good news of the gospel in word and deed.

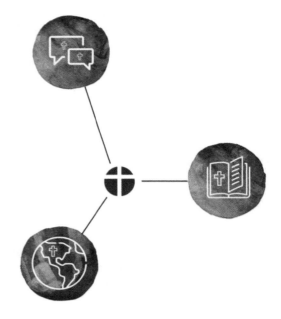

How to Use This Study

This Bible-study book includes seven weeks of content for group and personal study.

Group Study

Regardless of what day of the week your group meets, each week of content begins with the group session. Each group session uses the following format to facilitate simple yet meaningful interaction among group members and with God's Word.

Introducing the Study & Setting the Context
These pages include **content and questions** to get the conversation started and **infographics** to help group members see the flow of the biblical storyline.

Continuing the Discussion
Each session has a corresponding **teaching video** to help tell the Bible story. These videos have been created specifically to challenge the group to consider the entire story of the Bible. After watching the video, continue the **group discussion** by reading the Scripture passages and discussing the questions on these pages. Finally, conclude each group session with **a personal missional response** based on what God has said through His Word.

Personal Study

Three personal studies are provided for each session to take individuals deeper into Scripture and to supplement the content introduced in the group study. With **biblical teaching and introspective questions**, these sections challenge individuals to grow in their understanding of God's Word and to respond in faith.

Leader Guide

A tear-out leader guide for each session is provided on pages 95-108, which includes possible answers to questions highlighted with an icon and suggestions for various sections of the group study.

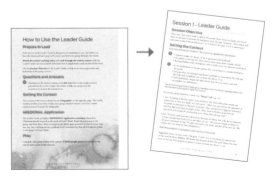

God's Word to You

A Life Worth Dying For

In the beginning, God created all things good. With the making of humankind as male and female, He even declared His creation to be very good. Paradise was the location; abundant life was the experience, that is, until the taint of sin covered the world through the rebellion of Adam and Eve against their Creator.

As a result, humanity lost its paradise and was separated from the God who created all things good. Death was God's warning for disobedience, and death became the reality—the death of living apart from God (sin), the death of life (physical death), and the death of eternal separation from God's goodness (spiritual death).

But the God of all good things was not finished. He called a people to Himself to be a light to the world. He gave them His holy expectations that they should follow them. He made provision for sin through sacrifices. And even when His people continued to rebel against Him, He promised life from death.

In comes Jesus, the Son of God sent into the world to make all things new. "In him was life, and that life was the light of men" (John 1:4). "Full of grace and truth," Jesus obeyed all of the Father's holy expectations (1:14). He is the "Lamb of God, who takes away the sin of the world!" (1:29). He laid down His life in death on a cross to secure life for those who follow Him (10:11), and He proved it in His resurrection when He took up His life again (10:18). A thief comes to steal, kill, and destroy; Jesus came so we might once again have life and have it in abundance (10:10).

So how should we respond to this good news? By turning from sin (repentance) and believing in Jesus (faith). "The one who loves his life will lose it, and the one who hates his life in this world will keep it for eternal life" (12:25). The treasures and pleasures of this world cannot compare to the eternal life found in Jesus.

God Hears His People

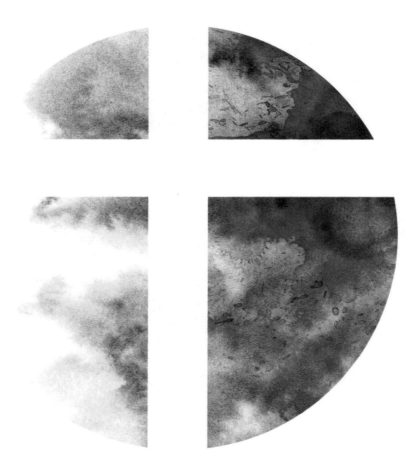

Introducing the Study

The God who spoke the cosmos into existence is the faithful God who keeps His promises to His people. He is faithful despite His people's unfaithfulness to Him. Humanity continued to sin against God and wander from Him, yet God would not abandon His promise to rescue and redeem people from slavery to sin and death.

What are some ways you have seen God pursue you?

This God who rescues people from sin is the same God who heard the cries of His enslaved people in the Old Testament. When the children of Israel cried out in despair from bondage in Egypt, God heard them, not because of their faithfulness or righteousness but instead because of the covenant He had made with Abraham. In the same way, we can rest assured that God hears our cries because of His faithfulness, not ours. God is with us in all circumstances and will not abandon us in our sinful state. Instead, He has actively intervened in history, through Jesus, to provide the way of redemption.

Do you think most people have a sense that they need to be rescued from their sin? Why or why not?

Setting the Context

Through the many ups and downs of his life, **God used Joseph** to sustain his family. Joseph rose to great power in the foreign land of Egypt, and when a great famine struck the region, his family found the help they needed to survive in their long-lost brother. The family of Israel, numbering seventy, moved to Egypt, but before long, the Israelites were so numerous that Egypt was filled with them. A new king then rose to power in Egypt and began to oppress them, **enslaving them into forced labor**.

 How does slavery serve as an appropriate metaphor for the curse of sin and death in this world?

So, God's chosen people, the bearers of His covenant with Abraham, lived in Egypt for four hundred years as slaves. Because they continued to multiply, Pharaoh ordered every male baby of Israelite birth be thrown into the Nile. One Israelite mother hid her son in her home as long as she could. When she could no longer do so, **she put her son in a basket and floated him down the Nile** in faith that somehow he would be saved.

As God would have it, Pharaoh's own daughter found the basket and named the boy **Moses**. He lived as her son in the palace until one day he sought to defend his people. He killed an Egyptian taskmaster but then ran for his life into the land of Midian, where he lived as a shepherd for forty years, not knowing that he would play a crucial part in God's plan of deliverance. **"Moses' Life"** (p. 11) provides a quick overview of Moses' part in God's plan.

 How can past experiences of God's faithfulness increase our hope in His future deliverance?

✝ CHRIST Connection

God told Moses His name "I AM" as a revelation of His transcendent self-existence. Jesus is the eternal Son of God, the great "I AM," who came to save us from sin.

Moses' *Life*

0–40

A Son in Egypt
- Born; placed in a basket in the Nile River; found by Pharaoh's daughter (Ex. 2)
- Killed an Egyptian taskmaster beating a Hebrew slave (Ex. 2; cf. Acts 7:23-24)
- Fled to Midian (Ex. 2)

40–80

A Shepherd in Midian
- Married Zipporah and had a family (Ex. 2)
- Met with Yahweh at the burning bush (Ex. 3–4; cf. Acts 7:30)

80–120

A Prophet for God
- Returned to Egypt to confront Pharaoh with the plagues (Ex. 4–12)
- Led the Israelites in the exodus and crossing the Red Sea (Ex. 12–14)
- Led the Israelites to Mount Sinai (Ex. 15–19)
- Gave the people God's law and His instructions (Ex. 20–Num. 10)
- Led the Israelites to southern edge of the promised land (Num. 10)
  – The people rebelled; condemned to wilderness for 40 years (Num. 13–14)
- Disobeyed God in how he brought forth water from a rock (Num. 20)
- After 40 years, led the Israelites to eastern edge of promised land (Num. 22)
- Allowed to see the promised land but not enter it (Deut. 3)
- Died on Mount Nebo (Deut. 34)

Continuing the Discussion

▶ Watch this session's video, and then continue the group discussion using the following guide.

In what ways are we, or have we been, like the people of Israel, enslaved in bondage?

How should remembering that God has rescued us in Jesus affect the way we live our lives?

As a group, read Exodus 3:2-10.

✴ What is evident about the character of God from these verses?

Why do you think God reminded Moses that He is the God of his ancestors?

How do you think you would have responded had you been Moses?

Though it had been four hundred years, God had not forgotten His promise to His people. He remained the same God who called Abraham, and it was time for Him to intervene on behalf of His people. At times, we might be tempted to doubt or forget the promises of God, but we can know for certain that God has not forgotten about us.

As a group, read Exodus 3:11-15.

When have you felt like Moses, unqualified to do what you know God has called you to do?

✴ How might God's answers to Moses encourage you when you feel unqualified?

What is significant about God's revelation of His name?

Moses was asking the wrong question. The issue was not about Moses' identity; it was about God's. God's name is more than something to call Him; it is the revelation of His character. Through this name, God was helping Moses see that He is present with and for His people at all times.

As a group, read Exodus 7:14-18.

These verses contain just one of several signs God gave through Moses. Why do you think God chose to deliver His people using signs like these?

✳ What would these signs have demonstrated both to God's people and the Egyptians?

Should we as God's people still expect signs like these? Why or why not?

In performing these signs and wonders, God demonstrated His power over all false gods. Each one of the signs He performed targeted a particular god that the Egyptians worshiped. In this case, the Egyptians worshiped the Nile, and God showed His power over that god. Ultimately, the greatest sign and wonder God performed was raising Jesus from the dead, proving that Jesus is Lord even over death.

✛ MISSIONAL Application

Record in this space at least one way you will apply the truth of Scripture as a believer in the sovereign God who hears His people.

Personal Study 1

God listens to the cries of His people.

Read Exodus 3:2-10.

It's a simple statement but often one difficult to believe: God listens to the cries of His people. When circumstances mount against us, when the pain in our lives is very real, we might wonder if God really hears our prayers and cries for help. This is surely what the Israelites felt throughout their protracted slavery in Egypt.

Moses, as an Israelite, was likely familiar with the cries of his people that had been offered up to God for four hundred years. The Israelites knew their history, that God had promised their forefather Abraham that He would give them a land of their own and He would bless them in a special way. Perhaps after so many years in slavery, some within the Israelite community wondered if God had gone back on His word.

Despite the decades and centuries that passed, God was still listening. In His mercy, God heard the cries of His people and responded. Notice who initiated the conversation: God came to Moses. God revealed Himself to the man He had chosen to intercede for His people and then identified Himself as the God of Moses' forefathers.

Humans have no right to demand an audience with God. God is not dependent upon us; all of creation is dependent upon Him. God is not accountable to us; we are accountable to Him. God would have been fully just and righteous to create this world and leave it to the natural processes He sustains, never to intervene (by way of a miracle), never to communicate with His human creatures (by way of special revelation), and never to involve Himself with our human plight (by way of redemption). There is nothing about our existence that forces God to be a God who reveals Himself. And yet, God listens to our cries and then acts in response.

God would not allow His people to continue to suffer. Instead, He would intervene to rescue them. Here we see a shadow of the good news of the gospel! The gospel is the story of a God who issues a call to helpless sinners. In our spiritual blindness and deafness, we are imprisoned and enslaved by our own sinfulness. We cannot see the goodness of God until He gives us new eyes. We cannot hear the voice of God until He opens our ears.

But God, out of sheer grace, spoke to us in a most unexpected way—through His Son, the Word. God chose to enter our world of darkness through the person of Jesus Christ. John 1 says, "In the beginning was the Word, and the Word was with God, and the Word was God" (v. 1). And then, "The Word became flesh and dwelt among us" (v. 14). Jesus is God's Word to us, breaking through our dark, silent prison and saying, "Let there be light!" ("In him was life, and that life was the light of men. That light shines in the darkness, and yet the darkness did not overcome it" [vv. 4-5].) In His perfect life and sacrificial death, Jesus revealed God to us. He showed us God's character. He demonstrated the love at the heart of the Father's authority.

This same heart of love, grace, and compassion is on display as God listened to the cries of His people. Just as He would later do in the gospel, God would take action on behalf of the Israelites. He would do for them what they could not do for themselves—bring them into freedom and, in so doing, continue to keep His covenant promise to Abraham.

What have you experienced or are you experiencing that might make you doubt whether God is listening to your cries?

How can reminding yourself of the gospel also remind you that God is indeed hearing you when you cry out to Him?

Personal Study 2

God reveals His character.

Read Exodus 3:11-15.

In the Old Testament, a name was much more than the means by which you could address someone. A name was a description of a person's character.

Even at this relatively early point in the Bible's story, we've seen the significance of names many times. God had already changed the names of Abram, Sarai, and Jacob. When they encountered God, the fabric of their identities was altered and God signified this change by changing their names. But while we have seen the importance of the names of people, we have not seen the importance of God's name to this point. Even in the foundational covenants God established with Noah and Abraham (Gen. 9:9; 17:2,7), He never explained the meaning of His name—"the LORD," or "Yahweh." Then came Moses' dramatic encounter with Yahweh at the burning bush.

Having been raised in the epicenter of Egypt, Pharaoh's house, Moses knew about the many gods of that ancient land, each with a name revealing something about him or her. Among these were Horus, the falcon-headed god of the sky and the pharaohs; Isis, the goddess of magic, motherhood, and fertility; and Ra, the sun god and creator. But what was the meaning of the name *Yahweh*?

There was good reason for Moses' question about God's name. Though the Israelites were already familiar with the name Yahweh (Gen. 12:8; 26:25; 28:13), they had been enslaved for centuries without any word from this God. Perhaps Moses was voicing the curiosity of many of his kinsmen when he asked the Lord about His name, wondering, "What does Your name signify?" In other words, Moses was asking in light of these long years of suffering, "Who are You?"

Perhaps you can identify with that. Perhaps you too know the feeling of reading in the Bible the promises of God to the believer in Christ and then looking closely at your life circumstances and wondering who is this God who would make such claims. It's during such times when we also might look to God and ask about His true identity: "Are You really the God I've read about? Are You really the God who promises never to leave or forsake me? Are You really the God who works all things for good?"

Yahweh's reply to Moses in verses 14-15 points to His identity as the covenant-making and covenant-keeping God. The Lord had made an everlasting promise to Abraham that he would be the father of many nations (Gen. 17:4). God had also told Abraham that his descendants would be enslaved for four hundred years but that He would set them free from slavery (Gen. 15:13-14). Now to Moses, God expressed that the meaning of the name Yahweh would be connected forever with His fulfilling the covenant promises made to Abraham, Isaac, and Jacob.

Even though Yahweh appeared in connection with a burning flame in a bush, He revealed Himself to Moses as a personal Being, not an abstract force. God makes promises and then He keeps them. He is "to be remembered in every generation" by the name Yahweh, the covenant-keeping King of His people who is always true to His word. This is His name, and His name can be trusted.

What do God's actions in relation to the covenant teach us about His character?

How does God's mission to rescue His people display His attributes?

Personal Study 3

God confronts false gods.

Read Exodus 7:14-18.

Having revealed His name to Moses and sent him as His emissary to Pharaoh, God was ready to confront the false gods of the Egyptians and to reveal His glory to everyone living in that land. God's judgment on the Egyptians through a series of severe plagues unfolds in the chapters that follow. Someone reading these passages today might look at these plagues and say, "Are you kidding me? This is bizarre! Is God a cosmic jerk? Was He just trying to annoy the Egyptians?" Or perhaps readers might merely roll their eyes and say, "This is absurd. Miraculous plagues? Really? That is hard to believe."

The series of plagues certainly was strange and severe. But we must understand that there's something bigger going on than what we see at first glance. God was judging not only the Egyptians but also the gods of Egypt. In Exodus 12:12, God said that He was going to perform the last sign, the death of the firstborn, and in so doing, He would "execute judgments against all the gods of Egypt" (see also Num. 33:4).

The plagues fell on all the areas of life that were supposed to have been protected by Egypt's gods. God put His glory on display by judging these false gods—He alone is the Almighty. And God's first display of superior power was appropriate: a miracle on the Nile River.

The Nile was the lifeblood of Egypt. Essentially, Egypt didn't exist without the Nile. It was responsible for transportation, irrigation, water, food, and the setting of the calendar. This type of catastrophe would be similar to cutting off all oil supplies, the stock market collapsing, drinking contaminated water, and having no food in the grocery store. It would be total chaos. It's no surprise that the Egyptians worshiped the Nile as their creator and sustainer. At least three deities were associated with the Nile. But God totally humiliated these gods when He turned the mighty Nile into blood (see also Ps. 78:44; 105:29; Rev. 16:3-7).

The Pharaoh's magicians somehow replicated the miracle. But the fact that the people were digging for water shows that while they repeated the sign, they couldn't cleanse the water of the Nile. Still, Pharaoh refused to humble himself before the one true God (Ex. 7:23).

If you glance at the plagues following this one, you'll notice four recurring elements throughout the ten plagues (in general, not in each and every case):

1) The obedience of Moses and Aaron

2) God's superior power over Egypt's gods

3) Satan's counterfeits

4) The perpetual hardening of Pharaoh's heart

But there's one dominant theme: "You will know that I am the LORD" (see Ex. 7:17; 8:10,22; 9:14,16,29; 10:2). God let everyone know that He alone is God. We must not miss this overarching theme in the midst of all the details of the plagues: God's mission is to be known and worshiped.

Because God's mission is to be known and worshiped, this must also be the mission that drives our lives. Just as God would use these signs and wonders to deliver His people from the physical slavery of the Egyptians, so also has He used the wondrous resurrection of Jesus from the dead to deliver us from slavery to sin and death. Now, as His rescued people, we are tasked to seek both the physical and spiritual deliverance of others. We are to work for justice and mercy in physical, tangible ways in the world, all the while preaching the good news of spiritual freedom that can only come through Christ. As we do this, we are declaring the dominance of God over any false gods the world has to offer.

What are the false gods our society turns to for security?

How does God stand over against these false gods in judgment?

God Delivers His People

Introducing the Study

God had not forgotten His people or His promise to them. He revealed Himself to Moses and sent him as His representative to confront Pharaoh and all the false gods of the Egyptians. In doing so, God would rescue His people, but He would rescue them in a way that highlighted His great power and glory.

 Why is it important for us to note that God rescued His people in a way that brought Him glory?

The deliverance had begun, but the hardhearted Pharaoh was not ready to let the people of God go and worship Him. Time and time again, Pharaoh promised to let Israel go, only to go back on his promise and keep them in captivity. And each time, God would bring more judgment on the land. As the conflict rose to a crescendo, God would perform one final wonder that would not only secure the release of His people but would be a powerful pointer to the greater deliverance to come in Christ.

Have you ever participated in or learned about the Passover meal? If so, what was your experience like?

Setting the Context

"Let My people go!" This was the message God tasked Moses to deliver to Pharaoh. Along with that message, God promised Moses that He would bring about **great acts of judgment** upon the land of Egypt.

> When you think about God delivering His people from Egypt, what images come to your mind? Why?

The first of these judgments was turning the Nile into blood, followed by the swarming of frogs, gnats, flies, the death of all the livestock in the field, festering boils on all the people and animals in Egypt, a deadly hail storm, a plague of locusts, and three days of darkness.

Despite the severity of these events, each time the people of God were spared. There was no darkness in their land, no hail fell on the Israelites, and none of their livestock died. Yet **Pharaoh was unwilling** to recognize the authority God had over him. Though at times in the progression he tried to compromise with Moses and his God, ultimately he was never willing to do what the Lord told him to do.

Even after all the devastation on the land, there was **one more judgment** coming from God. This judgment would be so severe that Pharaoh would finally relent and God's people would go free. But this plague was also different from the ones before in that a Passover lamb was required for the Israelites to be spared. **"Seeing Jesus in the Exodus"** (p. 23) shows how this Passover lamb foreshadows Jesus Christ.

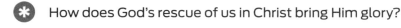 How does God's rescue of us in Christ bring Him glory?

✝ CHRIST Connection

Just as a spotless lamb was sacrificed to spare God's people from His judgment in Egypt, so also Jesus Christ is the Passover Lamb who was sacrificed to protect us from God's judgment of sin.

Seeing Jesus *in the* Exodus

OLD TESTAMENT	NEW TESTAMENT
Yahweh, the LORD "I AM" (Ex. 3:14-15)	**Jesus** "I AM" (John 8:58)
Moses A Mediator (Ex. 32:11-14)	**Jesus** The One Mediator (1 Tim. 2:5-6)
Moses A Prophet (Deut. 18:18-19)	**Jesus** The Prophet (Acts 3:22-26)
Israel, God's Firstborn Son Called Out of Egypt (Ex. 4:22-23)	**Christ, God's Firstborn Son** The Fulfillment (Matt. 2:15)
The Passover Lamb Protection from the Plague (Ex. 12)	**Christ, Our Passover** Purification from Sin (1 Cor. 5:7-8)

Continuing the Discussion

 Watch this session's video, and then continue the group discussion using the following guide.

How is Pharaoh's unwillingness to obey God a reflection of every human heart?

What are some specific ways the Passover foreshadows the death of Jesus Christ centuries later?

As a group, read Exodus 12:3-8,12-13.

What was the distinguishing characteristic that would keep God's people safe from the final plague?

Why is that an important detail for us to remember as Christians?

 What are some things we might be trusting in to keep us safe?

The Israelites would not be saved from the last plague by any other means except a lamb's blood on their doorposts. Just as they were saved by the blood of a lamb, so also are we saved by the blood of God's perfect Lamb, Jesus, who was sacrificed on our behalf. If we are trusting in any other means to keep us safe from God's judgment, then we are in the gravest of danger.

As a group, read Exodus 12:29-32.

 How do these verses reveal the severity of sin?

What similarities do you see between the world of the Egyptians and the world of today when it comes to God's judgment?

All the warnings were there. God had already demonstrated the seriousness of sin nine times, and yet, there were those who considered themselves safe from judgment. Likewise, the world today might discount the reality of God's judgment. It is our responsibility as Christians to sound the warning of what is to come and to share the true and only way of safety in Christ.

As a group, read Exodus 14:13-28.

> Is it surprising to you that the Israelites were so afraid, given what they had already witnessed? Why or why not?

✳ In what ways are we like the Israelites in this manner?

With the final plague, Pharaoh sent God's people away, but once again, he soon changed his mind. Pharaoh gathered his army and pursued the Israelites, but every battle does not belong to horses or chariots, and God had more than enough resources at His disposal to provide deliverance. Like the Israelites, we have borne witness to the power of God. Our past and ongoing deliverance from sin and death through Christ is the fuel for our confidence that God will keep us all the way to the end.

✠ MISSIONAL Application

Record in this space at least one way you will apply the truth of Scripture as a witness to the power and sovereignty of the one true God over all His enemies and false idols.

Personal Study 1

God delivers His people by providing a perfect sacrifice.

Read Exodus 12:3-8,12-13.

The plagues had wreaked havoc on the Egyptians, and God had manifested His glory in unleashing judgment upon the empire that stood against Him and His people. One final plague remained, one that would be worse than all the others. Not only would this plague be terrible in judgment, but it would be a lasting reminder to the Israelites.

God's people were to set apart a lamb for each household, or for the number of people who could eat a lamb (12:3-4). The lamb would serve as a substitute, dying in the place of each Hebrew firstborn son. However, the lamb was only acceptable if it was a one-year-old male without blemish (12:5). In Deuteronomy 17:1, God said that a blemished animal used for a sacrifice was an abomination. The Israelites needed a perfect substitute, a perfect sacrifice.

This need for a perfect sacrifice reminds us of our own state. Being corrupted by our sin, we cannot save ourselves. Our good works are like a blemished lamb, unworthy before a holy God. We need One who serves as a perfect substitute on our behalf. Jesus is the Lamb for the household of God. Only through faith in Him are our sins covered. He alone is our hope. Paul said, "For Christ our Passover lamb has been sacrificed" (1 Cor. 5:7).

In Exodus 12:6-7, we see what was to happen to this unblemished lamb. It was killed at twilight. The slain lamb vividly reminded everyone that all deserve judgment (see Rom. 3:23). Consequently, a blameless life had to be sacrificed in the place of the guilty people who needed salvation. The blood of the lamb was applied to the doorposts and lintel of the house (Ex. 12:7). The obedience of placing the blood on the doorway showed that you trusted God to keep His word and pass over you, sparing you and your family from judgment. So Israel escaped judgment through these sacrifices, and salvation for each family was accomplished by faith in the God who provided the substitute.

God was going to act decisively against the powerless gods of the Egyptians. Yahweh alone is to be feared, not Pharaoh! Only the Lord is the true, righteous Judge, and He will make Himself known. The events of Passover were an awesome demonstration of God's holy judgment on Egypt and their false gods.

The blood on the doorposts of the Israelites served as a sign that judgment had already fallen at that house. Just as the plagues were a sign to Egypt of God's justice and judgment, now the Passover was a sign of God's mercy to Israel. God would make a distinction with Israel, but this didn't mean that Israel was innocent. Israel wasn't innocent here because of their bloodline. They were judged as innocent because of the applied blood of the substitute. God judged Egypt, but He also judged Israel. The Passover demonstrated that apart from the blood of the lamb, Israel would be found guilty. Why? Because God is holy. All are sinners and deserve to be cut off from God. We are all like Pharaoh, even if we do not have the title. But God, in His grace, provides a way of salvation through the blood of a substitute—Jesus, the Lamb of God.

Why was it important that the sacrificial lamb be spotless? What did being spotless signify?

The blood on the doorposts was a public statement for all to see. How does this influence the way we think of our Christian faith?

What is the connection between our worship of the Lamb and our witness to the gospel?

Personal Study 2

God delivers His people by preserving life in the midst of judgment.

Read Exodus 12:29-32.

In this passage on the death of the firstborn, we see God's redeeming power displayed in a "great reversal." God began by striking down the firstborn sons of Egypt. He ended the debate regarding who is God with one cataclysmic sign. He judged all of Egypt without distinction, from rich to poor, king to slave. The cries in the land came from every family among the enemies of God. The destroyer went through the mightiest nation in the world and brought them to their knees.

Earlier, God told Moses, "And you will say to Pharaoh: This is what the LORD says: Israel is my firstborn son. I told you: Let my son go so that he may worship me, but you refused to let him go. Look, I am about to kill your firstborn son!" (Ex. 4:22-23). Here we see that God kept His word.

Through the tenth plague, God turned evil on its head. Pharaoh had enacted an unrighteous judgment on the Hebrew boys by throwing them in the Nile. Now, God enacted a righteous judgment on their sons. Pharaoh's judgment came back on him and his people.

In addition, by striking down the "gods" of Egypt, in particular, Pharaoh's son, God told Pharaoh that he wasn't a god and neither was his son. There's only one true God. This blow hurt Egypt not only personally through the loss of the son of succession but also theologically as God's power over their gods was displayed.

We should remember both the severity and the mercy of God. We all deserve this kind of judgment. We are all like Pharaoh. Some think they will never be judged. They think they can spend their lives as little Pharaohs, piling up pyramids full of stuff, chasing fame, and refusing to bow down to the one true God. Sadly, they will end up much like Pharaoh, unless they look to God alone for mercy.

And God is gracious and kind, ready to shower His mercy freely on people, even in the midst of judgment. On that dark night in Egypt, God provided a way for the Israelites to be saved, and He still does with us today. The requirement then was the blood of a sacrifice, and it is today as well.

How should we respond to this story of the Passover? First, we must remember that true freedom comes in Jesus Christ, the Lamb of God who takes away the sin of the world (John 1:29). He's the Lamb who provides us with total perfection and protects us from God's judgment (1 John 2:2; 4:10). He is the spotless, unblemished Lamb, chosen before the foundation of the world (1 Pet. 1:19-20). He is the Lamb whose bones were not broken (John 19:33-36), the ultimate Lamb crucified during Passover (Matt. 26:17-32). This Lamb applies His blood to our account (2 Cor. 5:21). Trust in Him alone for salvation.

Second, we must worship the Lamb. If you have come to Him by faith, then you can sing the song of the redeemed (Rev. 5:11-14). Our Savior is worth all of our praise, both our verbal praise and the praise that comes from an obedient life.

Finally, we must tell the world about the Lamb. We should tell everyone about the judgment that is to come and offer to everyone the good news of salvation through Jesus, our substitute Lamb. Many around the world have yet to hear the good news.

What does the severity of God's judgment on Egypt say about His holiness and uniqueness as the one true God?

What are some ways we can be a light to the nations while proclaiming the glory of the Lamb?

Personal Study 3

God delivers His people by His power.

Read Exodus 14:13-28.

Exodus 14 records one of the most important stories in the Bible—the crossing of the Red Sea. God would get His people out of Egypt through the miracle of parting the sea, and He would judge the Egyptians by swallowing them up in the sea.

Yes, Pharaoh let the people go, but the danger was not over. The Israelites were barely out of sight when Pharaoh changed his mind and came after them. The Israelites found themselves caught between the worst kind of rock and hard place—the Red Sea on one side and the armies of Egypt on the other.

Moses obeyed the instructions God gave him (14:16,21), but think about these instructions. Pharaoh was coming, the people were terrified, and God said, "Hold up your stick, wave your hand, and I will part the waters!" Why? Once again, the theme of God's glory is repeated: "I will receive glory by means of Pharaoh" (14:17). It may have sounded foolish, but Moses obeyed.

God's deliverance manifested itself through the parting of the waters (14:21), and the Israelites walked through to safety on dry ground (14:22).

Can you imagine this? The water was pulled back to be a wall on their right and their left (14:22). The idea of a "wall" carries the idea of a "city wall." When we read this, we might think of Niagara Falls. It's massive. The parting of the waters, though, was not too hard for the Lord of all creation.

As the Egyptians pursued the Israelites between the walls of water, "the LORD looked down," majestically exalted above all (14:24). He threw the Egyptians into a panic and clogged the wheels of their fine chariots (14:24-25). They wanted to flee but they couldn't.

After Israel completed their crossing of the sea, Moses stretched out his hand once again so that the waters came down on the Egyptians and destroyed them. This was total elimination. At daybreak, the Israelites saw God's victory, for the Egyptians were swallowed up when the water went back into the gap (14:26-28).

Just as Moses led his people through the waters of judgment to the other side, those who are in Christ will safely pass through the waters of death to the other side because of His mighty resurrection. This is what baptism represents—passing from death to life. In baptism, we are saying, "I have died with Christ, I have been buried with Him, and I have been raised with Him!" (see Rom. 6:1-4).

The true story of the exodus provides a picture of what has happened to us in salvation and in the Christian life. This happens in the same way the Red Sea was parted— by the power and grace of God. The Israelites were delivered by God's power from bondage, through grace, by a mediator, just as we are in Christ.

In what ways have you seen the power of God after a season of waiting for God to act?

Why is it important that God's saving actions on our behalf demonstrate our weakness and His strength?

Why is it important that we give all glory and praise to God for His salvation rather than think we have contributed something?

God Establishes the Worship of His People

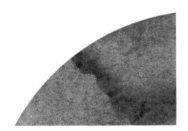

Introducing the Study

God's people were delivered from slavery and oppression, not because of their courage, commitment, or righteousness but instead by God's mercy. As judgment fell on Egypt, the people of Israel were saved through a sacrificial substitute. In the same way, we are only saved from the judgment of God through the sacrificial Lamb of God who takes away the sin of the world.

> **What are we tempted to trust in, besides God, for our future security?**

The people of God had witnessed the power of God deliver them, but God was just getting started in His renewed relationship with them. God has always desired to live in relationship with His people, both then and now, but His people need to be taught how to relate rightly to Him.

 Why is it comforting to know that God desires to live in relationship with His people?

Setting the Context

The people of God had been miraculously **delivered out of slavery**. They had experienced God's power and glory through the plagues on Egypt and the parting of the Red Sea. But despite these miracles, the people quickly grew **disgruntled** as they began the journey to the promised land.

> How should understanding God's judgment and our deliverance motivate us to live?

Though God had shown His power and willingness to provide for their needs, the people failed to trust in the manner of His provision. They **complained** about their lack of food and water, but the Lord, once again, was faithful to provide. God caused **manna**, a bread-like substance, to rain down from heaven each morning, providing sustenance for the people on a daily basis.

After three months, God brought the people to **Mount Sinai**, where they would worship Him. God met the people there, but they were terrified at His power displayed through thunder and lightning and a thick cloud on the mountain. God had told Moses to set a boundary around the mountain, knowing that because of their sin, the people could not come close to Him and live. But **God instructed Moses and gave him the law** so the people could know how to worship Him and live according to His commands. These instructions included building **"The Tabernacle"** (p. 35).

 How does the human response to laws reveal that the gospel is the only means by which we can live intimately with God?

✝ CHRIST Connection

The law reveals how we are to live properly in relationship with holy God and others, but because of sin, it is impossible to keep God's law. God sent His Son, Jesus, to "tabernacle," or dwell, with us, and through His life of perfect obedience, His death, and His resurrection, we are forgiven of our sin and credited with His righteousness when we trust in Him.

The **Tabernacle**

- God showed Moses the pattern for the tabernacle and all of its furnishings (Ex. 25:9).

- God filled Bezalel and Oholiab with wisdom and skill to complete the work and to teach others who also were given wisdom and skill for the construction of the tabernacle (Ex. 35:30–36:1).

- The people of Israel did according to all that the Lord had commanded Moses (Ex. 39:32).

Eden		The Tabernacle
Genesis 3:8	God's Presence	Exodus 40
Genesis 3:24	East-Facing Entrance	Numbers 3:38
Genesis 3:24	Guarded by Cherubim	Exodus 26:31-35 (Cherubim Embroidered in the Veil)
Genesis 2:9	Tree of Life	Exodus 25:31-40 (The Golden Lampstand)

Continuing the Discussion

 Watch this session's video, and then continue the group discussion using the following guide.

Why did God give the law if He knew in advance that His people would be unable to keep it?

How does the gospel change our perspective on the law given to God's people?

How should we as Christians view the Ten Commandments?

As a group, read Exodus 20:1-8.

What do these four commandments have in common, and why do you think they come first in the Ten Commandments?

How did Jesus interpret these commands in Matthew 22:34-40?

 What is the connection between obedience and love?

Everything in life begins with loving the Lord. When we love the Lord in the way He commands, obedience to the other commandments, including the commands that deal with our other relationships, flows naturally from that love. Jesus knew obedience begins in the heart, which is why He summarized all of God's law in terms of loving God and loving others.

As a group, read Exodus 20:12-17.

 How does the way we relate to others connect to our love of God?

Why must we understand the heart issues behind these commandments instead of viewing them as merely outward acts of obedience?

The law of God is not merely about external obedience; it is a command of love. This brings us face to face with the true human condition—our inability to change our own hearts. This is why we need the gospel. Only through the gospel can we have a new heart in Christ geared toward loving and obeying God.

As a group, read Exodus 40:34-38.

 How did God's presence benefit the people of God?

In what sense does God live among His people today?

What benefits does His presence bring to us?

God showed His desire to be among His people by filling the tabernacle with His glory. When the Holy Spirit came at Pentecost, God took up residence within every believer. The Christian is the new tabernacle in which the Spirit of God dwells, and we can trust Him for guidance, comfort, conviction, and empowerment to live out our gospel mission.

 MISSIONAL Application

Record in this space at least one way you will apply the truth of Scripture as a tabernacle for the Spirit of God in this world.

Personal Study 1

God gives the law to reveal how to worship and honor Him.

Read Exodus 20:1-8.

When we think of Moses on Mount Sinai, we think of the Ten Commandments. And we should, but it's important that we put these commandments in context. The two verses that introduce the Ten Commandments (Ex. 20:1-2) offer helpful insight as they reassure Israel of God's power and love, setting the stage for the commandments that follow. The Ten Commandments are not a list of rules from a rigid and uncaring taskmaster; they flow from the heart of our loving Father. But at the same time, God's love for us in no way compromises or diminishes His authority as Creator. God is all-powerful, as seen in how He rescued the Israelites from slavery in Egypt.

God was reassuring His people that He loved them enough to rescue them, and He had not forgotten them. The law He was about to give further emphasized His provision and care. While false religion frustrated people by keeping them guessing as to how to placate their imaginary gods, God loved His people enough to show Himself and His expectations in the law. By telling Israel about Himself through the law, God was establishing a clear understanding of how to know and please Him. The law removed any ambiguity and showed them what it looked like to apply God's holiness to their lives.

With the first commandment, God reminded Israel (and us) that He deserves our full devotion simply because of who He is. God has no rival, and He has called people to demonstrate their loyalty by giving no one and nothing else greater devotion than is given to Him. In the garden, Adam and Eve fell to the temptation to "be like God." In this first commandment, God turns right side up what was turned upside down by human sin. Giving God the place He rightly deserves in our affections is necessary for every action, thought, and relationship.

The second commandment amplifies the first. In our sin, we who are made in God's image turn around and seek to make Him into ours. We fashion idols and put our trust in them, hoping they will make us significant and bring us salvation. The desire to deify anything but God comes from a heart that is always striving to compete with God for first place. Left to our own devices, we will always choose to exalt ourselves and wrap our lives around things we believe will fulfill us.

Our hearts have to be remade and empowered by something outside of ourselves, something that can break our sinful tendency to worship things that are inferior to God. Only God can remake us, and He accomplishes this through Christ. Part of the law's function is to demonstrate the futility of our striving to follow God in our own power. We cannot elevate Him to His proper place in our lives without being born again through faith in Christ.

You and I may not struggle with making statues or images of gods to give our attention and devotion to, but we should be on guard for idolatry in its more subtle forms. An idol can be anything or anyone that we give first place to in our lives. The first two commandments and the others that follow remind us that God is a loving and jealous God who will tolerate no rivals to His throne. He must be first in our lives.

Is it possible to break one of the other commandments without breaking the first? Why or why not?

What are some of the good things in your life that you struggle against making into an idol?

How does the power of Christ help you keep these things in proper perspective?

Personal Study 2

God gives the law to reveal how to love one another.

Read Exodus 20:12-17.

Verse 12 serves as a hinge for the Ten Commandments. The first set of commandments deals directly with the way we love and honor God; this second set of commandments deals with our relationships with others. But we should be careful to understand how these two categories of commandments fit together. The Bible shows us over and over again that the way we treat others flows from our love for God. We cannot claim to love God if we aren't loving other people, and we cannot properly love other people apart from God's love saturating our minds and hearts. So when we come to these commandments, we should understand that although they might not explicitly address our relationship to God, they are nevertheless dependent upon it.

It makes sense that the fifth commandment, the hinge, would deal with the family since God created the family as the center of human relationships. God calls us to honor our parents in response to God's redeeming love for us. Though all human parents are sinful, God does not call us to weigh our parents' worthiness and then decide whether or not to honor them. He calls us to honor them as a way of honoring Him, of recognizing His authority in our lives.

The next commandment is clear and concise. Murder, and the motive that lies behind it, is condemned as a sin because of the way it disregards the inherent value of human life. When we judge a person's worth by any standard (such as intellect, ability, or our definition of "wholeness") instead of recognizing everyone is of equal worth as image-bearers of God, we are guilty of rejecting the inherent dignity the Creator has given us all. We steal God's right to ascribe value and claim that power for ourselves.

The prohibition against adultery is rooted in God's original design for sexual expression to be reserved for marriage. Adultery damages the family and destroys the sacred refuge God intends our homes to be. As harmful as these damages are, there is an even more important reason adultery is such a damaging sin. The marriage covenant is sacred and is an earthly picture of Jesus' relationship to His church. Jesus is the faithful, loving Bridegroom who has entered into an intimate bond with the people He has redeemed. Our marriages are intended to show the world a living object lesson of the love and faithfulness of Christ. Adultery destroys that picture.

The eighth commandment forbids stealing, which covers a wide range of dishonest practices all birthed in a heart gripped by possessions instead of the One from whom all good things come (Jas. 1:17). Anytime we deal dishonestly with others, cheat our employees or employers, or plagiarize, we engage in thievery. Our willingness to steal also betrays our lack of trust in the ongoing provision of God for our needs.

The ninth commandment forbids us to bear false witness against our neighbors. Throughout the Old Testament, God expressed His hatred for lying lips and declared truthfulness to be a requirement for His people (Ps. 5:6; Prov. 6:16-19; cf. Ps. 15). Because He is a God who tells the truth, His people must also tell the truth, always.

Regarding each of these commandments, Jesus would later in the New Testament deepen our understanding of them. In His teaching, Jesus made it clear that murder, adultery, theft, and lying are not merely physical acts of disobedience; the passions in the heart that fuel these actions are equally as sinful.

The long and short of it is that we need new hearts if we are to obey these commands. And the only way we can have new hearts is through the transformative power of the new birth in Jesus Christ.

Why is it important that we understand the full extent of these commandments—speaking to our sinful hearts, as Jesus taught?

Which of these commandments convicts you the most? Why?

Personal Study 3

God fills the tabernacle with His presence.

Read Exodus 40:34-38.

The Israelites left Egypt on the fifteenth day of their first month. They arrived at Sinai within a few weeks and shortly after that received the Ten Commandments (Ex. 19:1; Num. 33:3). They then received further laws and began constructing the tabernacle as God had commanded. At this point, almost a year had passed since the exodus.

When everything was ready, Moses caused the tabernacle to be set up "in the first month of the second year, on the first day of the month" (Ex. 40:17). The tent was erected in the center of the Israelite encampment, a pattern they would follow throughout their wilderness travels (Num. 2:2). Moses took the lead in consecrating—setting aside for its sacred purpose—each article of the tabernacle, anointing it with oil (Ex. 40:9-11). Aaron and his sons were similarly set apart as priests (40:12-15). Exodus 40 provides multiple reminders that Moses did everything concerning the tabernacle's dedication as the Lord commanded (40:16,19,21,23,25,27,29,32).

God had manifested His presence earlier to the Israelites in a pillar of cloud. A cloud was also visible over the temporary tent of meeting outside the Israelite camp, where Moses and the Lord talked (13:21; 33:7-11). But now something new and fantastic happened. God visibly showed up in the heart of the camp above the tabernacle, the newly constructed tent of meeting.

Twice in these verses "the glory of the LORD" is emphasized. The term translated "glory" carried ideas of both "weightiness" and "brightness." With reference to the God of Israel, glory referred to the overwhelming manifestation of His presence.

Ultimately, the brilliance within the tabernacle subsided so that the priests could fulfill their responsibilities inside the tent of meeting. The cloud, however, remained above the tabernacle as permanent evidence of God's presence in the Israelite camp.

The entire tabernacle section of Exodus, but particularly these concluding verses, proves conclusively that God wanted to be with His people, and He wanted them to know that He was with them. The same is true today. The greatest evidence of this truth is the incarnation—God Himself took on human form.

In Israel's history, the portable tabernacle was eventually followed by a permanent temple. Both structures were understood as the earthly dwelling place of the Lord. In fact, throughout the ancient world, a "temple" was a god's house. Israel's temple never had a physical image of God, as pagan temples did, but nevertheless functioned as the place, the sanctuary, where the Lord's holy presence was manifested.

The apostle Paul took up this language to remind early Christians, and us, that we are indwelt by God's Spirit. Therefore, we are God's temple, so we manifest His presence to others in the world. As Paul wrote: "Don't you yourselves know that you are God's temple and that the Spirit of God lives in you?" (1 Cor. 3:16). Here the "you" is plural, referring to believers collectively (see also 1 Cor. 6:19; Eph. 2:21-22). God's presence within each of us is what unites us together as one people in the name of Jesus Christ.

What does God's presence among the Israelites teach you about His desire to dwell among you and your fellow Christians?

Consider yourself as a mini-tabernacle. In what ways do you see God's glory in your life?

Is there any visible or sensory evidence of God's presence in and through you? Why or why not?

God's People Rebel

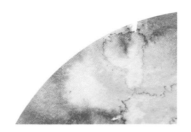

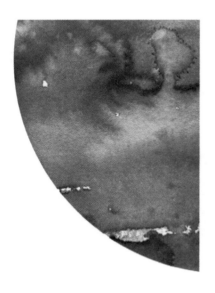
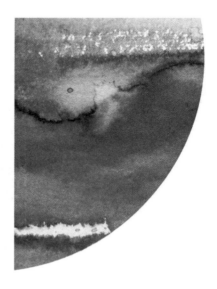

Introducing the Study

The Lord made it clear how His people were to worship and honor Him and relate to other people as fellow image-bearers of God. The clarity of God's law also revealed that because we are corrupted by sin, we can never keep it perfectly. The law, then, shows our desperate need for an answer outside of ourselves to our sin problem. We need Someone to live righteously on our behalf.

 Why must we see our inability to keep the law in order to come into a right relationship with God?

The law not only reveals our sin, it also reveals the perfect character of God. God requires righteousness for human beings to come into His presence because of His own holiness. But just as God's holiness runs through every part of His being, so also has sin tainted every part of the human experience.

Why is it right to say that every human was, at one time, a rebel at his or her core?

Setting the Context

The second half of **the Book of Exodus** shows the delivered people of God receiving instructions for how to live rightly with God and others. In **Leviticus and Numbers**, we see God expand on His law, reinforcing the fact that the people must come to God not on their terms but on His, for He is holy. In light of this, God gave instructions on worship, sacrifices, and job descriptions for different roles in the community.

 In what ways does the law point us to Christ?

But for all of God's provision, presence, and instruction, **the complaints of the people** that had begun so quickly after crossing the Red Sea began to grow louder, even coming from Aaron and Miriam, two pillars of the Israelite community and Moses' brother and sister. But the people were not merely grumbling against Moses; they were ultimately shaking their fists at God, the One who had appointed Moses and given him his authority. None of these grumblings escaped the Lord's notice or discipline.

> How does the goodness of God reveal the true evil of rebellion against Him?

"Journey to the Promised Land" (p. 47) shows that at long last, the people finally came to the edge of the land of Canaan, the land God had promised to their forefather Abraham. Standing on the southern edge of this land, the people now faced a choice. Would they trust God even in the face of adversity or would they turn back due to their lack of faith?

✝ CHRIST Connection

God's people rebelled against Him and refused to enter the land He had given them and grumbled about His provision, so He punished them for their continuing disobedience. Because of our sin, we too deserve to be punished by God, but He provided a way of salvation for us through Jesus. When we look with faith upon Jesus Christ lifted high on the cross, we are saved from the punishment of our sin.

Journey *to the* Promised Land

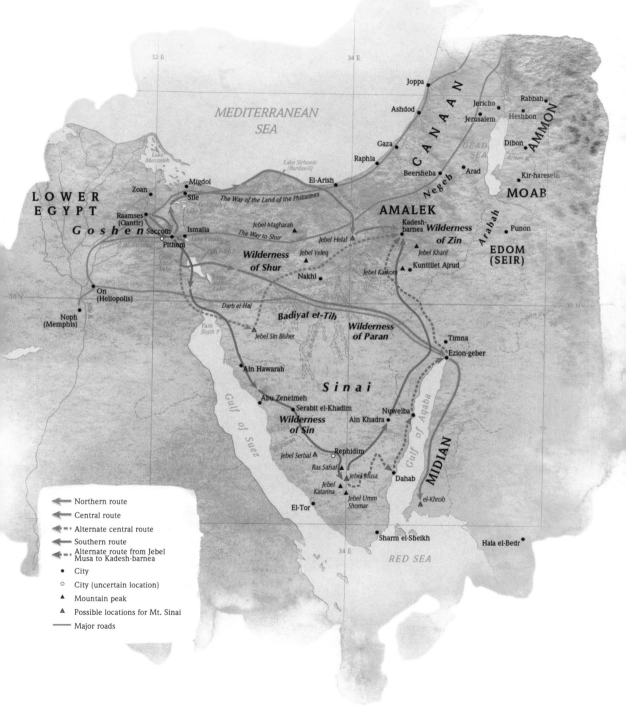

MEDITERRANEAN SEA

Joppa

Ashdod

Rabbah

Jericho
Jerusalem
Heshbon

AMMON

Gaza

DEAD SEA

Dibon

MOAB

Raphia

Beersheba
Arad

Kir-hareseth

Zoan

Migdol

El-Arish

CANAAN

Negeb

Sile

The Way of the Land of the Philistines

AMALEK

LOWER EGYPT

Raamses (Qantir)

Goshen

Succoth

Ismalia

Pithom

The Way to Shur

Kadesh-barnea

Wilderness of Zin

Jebel Magharah

Jebel Helal

Jebel Kharif

Punon

EDOM (SEIR)

Wilderness of Shur

Jebel Yeleq

Kuntillet Ajrud

Nakhl

Jebel Karkom

On (Heliopolis)

Darb el-Haj

30 N

Noph (Memphis)

Yam Suph?

Badiyat et-Tih

Jebel Sin Bisher

Wilderness of Paran

Timna

Ezion-geber

Ain Hawarah

Sinai

Abu Zenelmeh

Serabit el-Khadim

Nuweiba

Gulf of Suez

Wilderness of Sin

Ain Khadra

Gulf of Aqaba

MIDIAN

Jebel Serbal

Rephidim

Ras Safsaf

Jebel Musa

Dahab

Jebel Katarina

Jebel Umm Shomar

el-Khrob

El-Tor

Sharm el-Sheikh

Hala el-Bedr

RED SEA

Legend

← Northern route
← Central route
◄--- Alternate central route
← Southern route
◄--- Alternate route from Jebel Musa to Kadesh-barnea
• City
○ City (uncertain location)
▲ Mountain peak
▲ Possible locations for Mt. Sinai
— Major roads

Continuing the Discussion

▶ Watch this session's video, and then continue the group discussion using the following guide.

Why is sin not just a physical act but also an accusation against the character of God?

What are some responses people can make to God's offer of grace in the midst of judgment?

As a group, read Numbers 13:1-2,30-33.

✳ How is sin related to our faith?

Have you ever been in a situation like this, when it was difficult to exercise faith because of what your senses told you?

What are some promises of God that we need to remember when it is difficult to trust Him?

When the spies saw the size of the people in the land, their confidence in God evaporated. This is the beginning of rebellion, when we begin to doubt the provision and promises of God. Circumstances have a way of doing that; our senses tell us that what we know by faith cannot possibly be true. This is why the essence of faith is not in what we see but rather looking beyond what we see.

As a group, read Numbers 14:1-4,30-35.

✳ What lies about the character of God did the people believe here?

How might we be tempted to believe similar lies?

In what ways does sin always affect others beyond us?

Each sin we commit can be traced back to a failure to believe rightly about God. The children of Israel questioned God's love, wisdom, and power, leading to long-lasting consequences to the entire community. In this we see that though we might make a choice as an individual to sin, the consequences of sin always move beyond just ourselves and spill onto others.

As a group, read Numbers 21:4-9.

> Why were the complaints of the people so serious? What were they once again charging God with?

> How do you see both the justice and mercy of God in this account?

✳ How do these verses remind us of the gospel?

Judgment for sin is real, and the penalty for sin is death. But even in judgment, God is merciful to provide a way of salvation. The people were saved by gazing upon the bronze snake lifted up. In the same way, we can only be saved by turning toward Jesus, who was lifted up on a cross to pay the penalty for our sin.

✝ MISSIONAL Application

Record in this space at least one way you will apply the truth of Scripture as one who looks to Jesus in faith for salvation from sin and eternal life.

Personal Study 1

Rebellion begins by ignoring God's provision and promises.

Read Numbers 13:1-2,30-33.

The Lord once said to Abraham that He would make a great people of his descendants (the nation of Israel), give them a great land (Canaan), and provide great blessings for them and through them (Gen. 12:1-3). Centuries later, the Lord was ready to bring His people into that land, but they chose to focus on the apparent obstacles in their path instead of God's promises.

The spies who went into the land to scout it were not ordinary men. Instead, God wanted leaders from each tribe to do the reconnaissance work. They were to witness the goodness of God's provision in the land and report back to the people. Then acting on faith, the people would go forward to claim what God had promised.

The early part of the spies' report could be summarized like this: "It's better than you can possibly imagine!" The natural resources of the land were like nothing they had seen before. Having lived all of their lives in Egyptian slavery with a brief stint in the wilderness, such abundance was surely overwhelming, like being thrust into an American buffet restaurant. The abundant land given to Abraham was now available to the nation of his descendants.

But as is often the case in the Old Testament, the Israelites faltered in their faith. After describing the land as more than they had hoped for, the spies' report turned on its heels as they described why it was impossible to possess. Words like *large*, *strong*, and *fortified* were at the top of the spies' minds. They saw an unconquerable force before them. They took their eyes off the promise and put it on their enemies. By the end of the report, they weren't focusing on God's power or even the beauty of the land but instead were fixated on the perceived advantage of its inhabitants.

The spies had seen firsthand what they would have if the promise were fulfilled, but fear of the enemy caused them to lose their faith. They had let go of their identity as the people of God. They forgot who they were—the people of promise, saved by the one true God and commissioned to take the land God had for them. Instead, they looked at some really large soldiers and assessed themselves as "grasshoppers" in comparison (v. 33), as if they alone, without God, would have to win the victory.

"Like grasshoppers" was how they described themselves, but that was not how the Lord would describe them. To God, these people were His children delivered from slavery and ready to take hold of the land of promise. This shows us that the failure of faith is both losing faith in God's power and losing a sense of yourself as a child in God's story of redemption.

Only through faith in God and His work do we gain a true understanding of the world and ourselves. Because of Christ's redemptive work on our behalf, our identity has changed. We are no longer an enemy, an outsider, a rebel, or lost in the darkness. Instead, we are a member of God's family, His ambassador for Christ, a child of light.

In the face of the dangers present in the promised land, the spies lost their faith. Only Caleb and Joshua kept their faith and were ready to forge ahead, but they were outnumbered by their fellow spies, who believed the fortified cities were too great even for God to overcome.

What do you turn to for strength in moments when your faith is faltering? Why?

When have you faced a difficult circumstance similar to a time when God delivered you in the past?

Did reflecting on God's work in your life in the past give you strength for the present trial? Why or why not?

Personal Study 2

Rebellion impacts others and has consequences.

Read Numbers 14:1-4,30-35.

How did the people respond once their faith began faltering? They didn't reflect on what God had done in the past, neither did they look forward to God's future promise. They were overcome by the moment and paralyzed by their fear of death and despair.

When the leaders lost their faith, the people of Israel faced a crisis. Once the majority of spies said there was no hope, the Israelites went from wondering to mourning to outright rebellion. In the heat of the moment, the people's rebellion escalated. They took the position—which can only be described as ridiculous—that they would be better off dead! The people contemplated the merits of having died as slaves in Egypt or having died in the desert on the way to the promised land. They wanted the certainty of death over the possibility of death!

Here's a warning for us: The loss of faith includes a loss of sense. To wish for death when you are on the edge of God's promise is the result of a faithless heart.

Choosing slavery or death at the moment seemed a better option. They were ready to stone Moses, Aaron, Joshua, and Caleb to death and then try their luck crossing the wilderness back toward Egypt. Their choice was based on a lack of memory. All that God had done was somehow no longer in their mind. They forgot the power of God displayed in the past as well as the promise of God for their future.

The work of God in the past is not something only for the history books. It is the assurance of what He can do in your present circumstances. As the church, we must also look at our present circumstances from the viewpoint of God's work in the past and His promise for the future.

What's more, the choice to sin does not only affect us; there are others who have to face the consequences of our rebellion as well. This requires a shift in thinking for us because we tend to think of sin as something that we ourselves must deal with. We alone make the choice, and therefore, we alone bear the consequences.

But as we continue to read the account, we see that the consequences of the people's sin extended well beyond themselves to their children. This is the true way of sin. Though we might make a choice in isolation, there are others who will always feel the effect. For example, if we make the choice to engage in sexual immorality, our families will eventually feel the devastating effects. Or if we make the choice not to honor God with our money, the church will be limited in her ability to carry out God's mission. Such is the case with anger, bitterness, jealousy, and any other sinful pattern we develop.

Because our lives are naturally intertwined with the lives of others, our choices are never limited to us alone. They will always branch out into the lives of others, either for good or for ill.

When are your feelings and fears most likely to overwhelm your faith?

Can you see the effects of others' sin in your own family? How is that a sober warning to you?

Personal Study 3

Rebellion leads to punishment, but God provides a way of salvation.

Read Numbers 21:4-9.

The Israelite people had slavery behind them. But due to their unbelieving hearts, they had hardship before them. God wanted them to enter into the land that flowed with milk and honey. But the Israelites chose to believe in the overwhelming circumstances of the moment rather than in the sovereign God who guided them. The people wandered for forty years in the wilderness, but on the way, they were provided with everything they needed. Yet even after all this time, they spurned this gracious provision of God.

The people's rebellion in this instance shows up in a very simple word: impatient. The group of people who had been miraculously delivered, fed, and clothed by God now turned on Him. In essence, they threw a preschooler-like fit before God because they didn't like the food He provided.

The people went far beyond doubt. They accused God and Moses of treachery. They imagined God had intentionally led them out of Egypt for the express purpose of killing them in the desert. It was a rebellion of epic proportions. By stating such a claim, the people showed they doubted God's character and His word.

There in the wilderness, the people were replaying Adam and Eve's sin in the garden. Eve gave in to the temptation to doubt God's truthfulness. Furthermore, she doubted that the Lord had her best interests in mind. The Israelites put themselves in the same position. Their impatience revealed a lack of trust in God's goodness.

In response to their rebellion, God acted quickly and punished them. It was the type of punishment that would strike fear into the heart of any person. Suddenly, poisonous snakes were in the camp. Biting. Infecting. Killing. Modern-day readers may find it difficult to read about the punishment delivered against sin, but Scripture is clear: Because God is committed to redeeming and restoring all things, sin must be punished and wiped out. Events like this remind us of the costly nature of sin. The Israelites had to learn once again that sin leads to death.

Once God heard the people's penitent cry, He provided a way of restoration through their faith. In an act of divine irony, God instructed Moses to make a serpent of bronze and place it on a pole. If those bitten by the snakes on the ground would look to the snake that had been lifted up, they would be healed.

The word for "looked" in Hebrew does not mean a casual gaze or a quick glance. Rather, it indicates fixing your gaze upon something or to look intently. The Israelites would have to concentrate their mind's attention and heart's affection on God's provision. And this is precisely the way we receive mercy today for our own rebellion.

We do not fix our gaze on a bronze snake, but we do fix our eyes on something else lifted up—the cross where Jesus hung. Only through turning our attention to the cross and understanding that Jesus died in our place can we be cured of the poisonous sin that runs through every part of who we are.

God chose the symbol of their punishment for sin as the instrument of His mercy. Similarly, the cross, a symbol of guilt and shame, becomes an instrument of God's mercy for us.

What is the significance of God's command to the people to gaze at the snake?

What truths were the people to consider?

God Gives His People the Promised Land

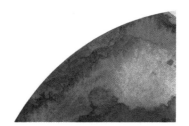

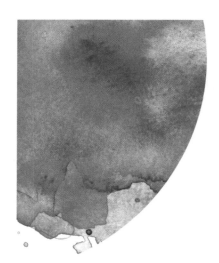

Introducing the Study

Rebellion is at the heart of every human being. Despite the good provision and promises of God, it is our natural inclination to spurn Him as our Lord and seek to live on our own terms. Because of this, we, like the Israelites, are deserving of God's divine judgment and in need of His mercy.

 How might we be tempted to complain about the provision of God?

Despite our rebellion, God's mercy and grace are never-ending. Just as God promised to fight on behalf of the Israelites if they would only trust in Him, so has He also fought the terrible enemies of sin and death on our behalf—and won through the death and resurrection of Jesus.

How should the fact that God has and will fight for us impact the way we live each day?

Setting the Context

The God of Abraham, Isaac, and Jacob keeps His promises. Just as He promised Abraham a land that would belong to his descendants, He promised those rebellious descendants that they would **wander for forty years** in the desert until the entire generation had died off. That's precisely what happened.

 What are some of the patterns that reveal our failure to trust in God's ability and willingness to fight for us?

Throughout those years, the Lord continued to lead His people through **Moses**. But like the rest of his generation, Moses rebelled against God in the Wilderness of Zin. As a result of his sin, Moses would not be the one to lead them into the promised land.

It was time for a new leader to emerge—**Joshua**, son of Nun. Joshua had been a military commander for the Israelites. He was also one of the two spies who trusted the Lord to give the Canaanites over to them, despite seeing their great size and strength. Further, Joshua had accompanied Moses as he spoke with God. So at God's command, Moses, before he died, conferred authority onto Joshua as the new leader over Israel.

With a new generation and a new leader, the Israelites stood on the brink of the promised land once again, and the choice of whether or not they would trust God to fight for them was once again before them. **"Conquest of the Promised Land"** (p. 59) shows that for the most part, they did.

What are some ways you have learned from the mistakes your parents made? What are some ways you follow in their steps?

CHRIST Connection

The Valley of Achor is a chilling reminder of sin and its consequences, but God later promises to make the Valley of Achor "a gateway of hope" (Hos. 2:14-15). The wages of sin is death, but the gift of God is eternal life through Jesus Christ our Lord, who has won our victory through His faithful obedience.

Conquest *of the* Promised Land

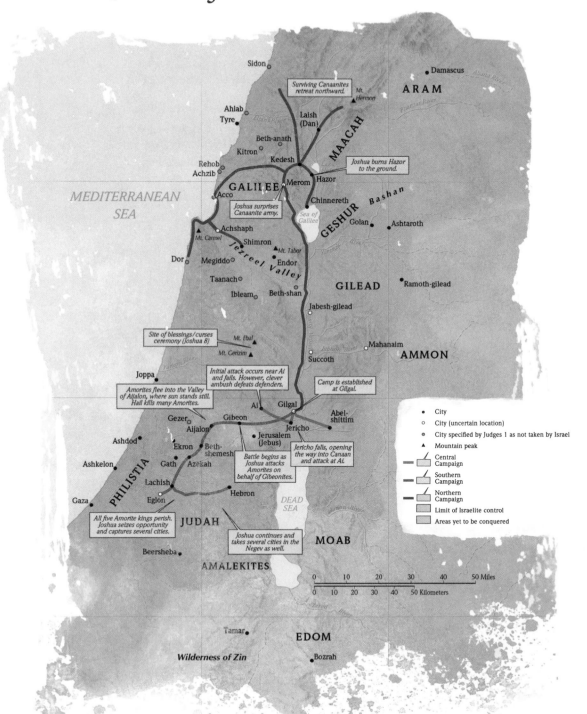

Sidon

Damascus

ARAM

Surviving Canaanites retreat northward.

Mt. Hermon

Ahlab

Tyre

Laish (Dan)

MAACAH

Beth-anath

Kitron

Kedesh

Rehob

Achzib

GALILEE

Merom

Hazor

Joshua burns Hazor to the ground.

MEDITERRANEAN SEA

Acco

Chinnereth

Sea of Galilee

GESHUR

Bashan

Joshua surprises Canaanite army.

Golan

Ashtaroth

Achshaph

Mt. Carmel

Shimron

Mt. Tabor

Dor

Megiddo

Jezreel Valley

Endor

GILEAD

Ramoth-gilead

Taanach

Ibleam

Beth-shan

Jabesh-gilead

Site of blessings/curses ceremony (Joshua 8)

Mt. Ebal

Mt. Gerizim

Succoth

Mahanaim

AMMON

Joppa

Initial attack occurs near Ai and fails. However, clever ambush defeats defenders.

Camp is established at Gilgal.

Amorites flee into the Valley of Aijalon, where sun stands still. Hail kills many Amorites.

Ai

Gilgal

Abel-shittim

Gezer

Gibeon

Jericho

Aijalon

Jerusalem (Jebus)

Jericho falls, opening the way into Canaan and attack at Ai.

Ashdod

Ekron

Beth-shemesh

Gath

Azekah

Battle begins as Joshua attacks Amorites on behalf of Gibeonites.

Ashkelon

PHILISTIA

Lachish

Gaza

Eglon

Hebron

DEAD SEA

All five Amorite kings perish. Joshua seizes opportunity and captures several cities.

JUDAH

Joshua continues and takes several cities in the Negev as well.

MOAB

Beersheba

AMALEKITES

Tamar

EDOM

Wilderness of Zin

Bozrah

- • City
- ○ City (uncertain location)
- ◎ City specified by Judges 1 as not taken by Israel
- ▲ Mountain peak
- Central Campaign
- Southern Campaign
- Northern Campaign
- Limit of Israelite control
- Areas yet to be conquered

| 0 | 10 | 20 | 30 | 40 | 50 Miles |

| 0 | 10 | 20 | 30 | 40 | 50 Kilometers |

Continuing the Discussion

 Watch this session's video, and then continue the group discussion using the following guide.

Why do you think the people were willing to go forward at this moment when their parents turned back forty years prior?

How can conquering the promised land be consistent with God's promise to bless all the nations of the earth through Abraham's descendants?

As a group, read Joshua 6:1-5.

Put yourself in the place of Joshua. How might you have reacted when you heard God's plan for conquering Jericho?

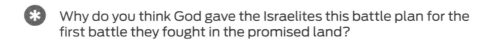 Why do you think God gave the Israelites this battle plan for the first battle they fought in the promised land?

What was God demonstrating to His people, and to the people inhabiting the promised land, through the battle of Jericho?

It must have been a strange battle plan for Joshua, a military leader. Based on how many times he had heard the phrase "Be strong and courageous" repeated, perhaps Joshua even wondered about the wisdom of such a plan. But God wanted to demonstrate for His people that He would fight for them if they would only trust. Further, He wanted the battle to be won in a way that would bring all the glory to Himself.

As a group, read Joshua 7:1-12,24-26.

 What does this account show you about the destructive nature of sin?

How does this story serve as a warning for us?

Compared to Jericho, the conquest of Ai should have been easy. But the sin of one man, Achan, led to defeat instead of victory. Achan's sin reminds us that sin is never truly secret, and it's never truly without consequence both to us and to those closest to us. God will not leave sin unpunished and will, in His time, set all accounts right.

As a group, read Joshua 8:1-2.

 What is encouraging about this word from the Lord, especially in light of Israel's previous defeat?

Why might that encouragement be comforting to the Christian today?

God will not leave sin unpunished, but God is also willing to deal with sin and move on. This is immensely encouraging for Christians today because we can trust that our sin has indeed been dealt with by Jesus and that God is not keeping a record of our wrongs.

✝ MISSIONAL Application

Record in this space at least one way you will apply the truth of Scripture as a strong and courageous believer in Jesus Christ, who fights His enemies on behalf of His people.

Personal Study 1

God gives His people victory over their foes.

Read Joshua 6:1-5.

At the start of Joshua 6, we know that God has promised victory in the promised land. But the plan He revealed for the first battle had no logical rationale. It offered no assurance of a military conquest. It had nothing to do with military might, and it did not include common weapons of warfare.

The city of Jericho was locked down. Its gates were shut up tightly because the inhabitants were fearful of Joshua and the Israelites. No citizen of Jericho was allowed to exit the city, and the king of Jericho and his army were preparing to prevent the Israelites from entering the city.

In chapter 2, the narrator allows us to hear the words of Rahab the prostitute, who told the Israelite spies, "When we heard this, we lost heart, and everyone's courage failed because of you, for the LORD your God is God in heaven above and on earth below" (Josh. 2:11). The God who fights for Israel has a master key to every door in the universe and can open doors that are closed (Rev. 3:7)—even those in Jericho. That's why we see the Lord reiterating in Joshua 6 what He said generally in Joshua 1:3: "I have given you every place where the sole of your foot treads, just as I promised Moses."

But what a strange battle plan! How could marching around the wall of Jericho one time for each of six days and seven times on the seventh day ever bring down the massive wall that was wide enough, according to the ancient historian Josephus, for two chariots to ride on it side by side without falling over? Can you imagine the priests as they listened to Joshua give God's instructions? They probably wondered if Joshua was hearing God as well as Moses had heard Him. Surely Joshua missed a portion of God's instructions!

God gave Joshua a military formation that seemed to make them an easy target for Jericho. Military personnel comprised the vanguard. Directly behind them were seven priests blowing a ram's-horn trumpet. Positioned behind these were priests carrying the ark of the covenant (representing the presence of God in the midst of His people). The rearguard was stationed behind the priests who carried the ark of the covenant. And in this way, they marched around the wall of Jericho.

God used a seemingly foolish battle plan to accomplish His purpose: "God has chosen what is foolish in the world to shame the wise, and God has chosen what is weak in the world to shame the strong" (1 Cor. 1:27). But throughout this action plan, we see that the Israelites must be involved. God would execute what the Israelites implemented. God's people had to participate in the battle of Jericho by marching around the wall, and God would give them victory by bringing down the wall.

God told Joshua that at the conclusion of their last trip around the wall, the priests would make an extended blowing of the trumpet, which would be followed by the shouting of the entire army. God's unconventional battle plan showcased trumpet blowing preceding shouts, and the action would begin with a few and then spread to the rest of the people. Consequently, Jericho would experience a catastrophic event—the wall would collapse. This thick wall would implode upon itself without a bulldozer or a wrecking ball because God would bring it down. God's instructions, however, were not enough to bring down the wall. His plan required the Israelites to act in faith.

When God leads you in a specific direction, how do you hold fast to His instructions even when others doubt you have heard from God?

How do you weigh what you believe God is calling you to do with the doubts or concerns you hear from other people?

Personal Study 2

One man's sin leads to defeat for Israel.

Read Joshua 7:1-12,24-26.

In Joshua 6:27, we read: "And the LORD was with Joshua, and his fame spread throughout the land." But chapter 7 opens with a change-of-direction conjunction—"The Israelites, however, were unfaithful regarding the things set apart for destruction." A change-of-direction conjunction indicates whatever happened before will now be different. Whenever you see a "however" or a "but" in Scripture, it's usually a good thing when it comes before God, and usually a bad thing when it comes after God.

In this text, the change-of-direction conjunction is a bad sign because it comes after a statement about how the Lord was with Joshua. Joshua sent some spies to the city of Ai, just as he sent two spies to collect intelligence on Jericho (Josh. 2:1). He was preparing to take the next steps in his quest to conquer Canaan and knew he could not attack the larger cities of Canaan without being seen by Ai. He needed to conquer Ai to maintain an element of surprise.

The spies returned with a jubilant (and somewhat arrogant) recommendation. According to them, the battle would be a piece of cake. Joshua usually received his marching orders from the Lord: from how the Israelites were to march across the Jordan River to how they were to march around the wall of Jericho. But this time, he quickly accepted the recommendation and deployed three thousand men to fight against Ai.

In a surprising turn of events, this small city put the Israelites on the run. Apparently, Israel had forgotten that it was not their army who defeated the much larger city of Jericho; it was the Lord who fought for them. They lost the battle at Ai because the Lord who had fought for them did not fight for them at Ai.

Joshua reacted to this shattering news by tearing his clothes and falling on his face before the ark of the Lord. In his prayer to God, Joshua sounded a lot like Moses (Ex. 32:12-13; Num. 14:13-16; Deut. 9:28), who was always concerned about God's reputation among the surrounding nations. Joshua knew that God had not brought the people into the promised land to abandon them. His knowledge of the God of his fathers led him to repent for the Israelites over the loss at Ai. Joshua knew God would not violate His trustworthy name.

The reason for Israel's defeat was the presence of rebellion in the camp. A man named Achan had sinned, and God associated Achan's individual sin with the entire community—God viewed it as a congregational transgression. God indicted the entire nation, and His anger was leveled against all Israel.

Sin is destructive. The sins of individual believers affect the family, the church, and the community. Perhaps others knew what Achan did and allowed it to persist. If they did, they affirmed him in his destructive actions. God told Joshua that He would not fight for him and the Israelites until the correction for their sin has been made.

Since all Israel was affected by Achan's sin, which resulted in the defeat of the nation and the loss of thirty-six lives, all Israel picked up stones to stone Achan and his family. The whole community took responsibility for ridding themselves of the accursed thing. We must also realize that in the church, we have a corporate responsibility for sin. We help each other follow Jesus, so we must call for confession of sin when we fail and fall.

Ever since Adam hid from God in the garden, we have been trying to hide our sin. What are some ways we can help each other bring our sin out into the open?

What happens when we minimize the horrible consequences of our sin?

Why does sin deserve death?

Personal Study 3

God gives His people victory after sin is dealt with.

Read Joshua 8:1-2.

Joshua 7 ends with these words: "Then the LORD turned from his burning anger." As frightening as the scene of Achan's punishment may seem, it later gives rise to a promise. God promised to one day "make the Valley of Achor into a gateway of hope" (Hos. 2:14-15). This place where Achan brought trouble upon Israel and then suffered the penalty of death for his sin would one day be a doorway to hope, because though the wages of sin is death, the gift of God is eternal life in Christ Jesus (Rom. 6:23).

Unlike Achan, who took unlawful things, Jesus Christ came to give the unthinkable—His life for ours (2 Cor. 5:21). Achan died for his sin so that the Lord's anger would turn from Israel. Jesus died for our sin so that we—who, like Achan, were enemies of God—could be reconciled to Him.

Though Joshua had uncovered the sin in the camp, he did not presume success on the battlefield. This time, He listened to the Lord about the number of soldiers who should fight against Ai. God instructed Joshua to take all the soldiers with him and go to Ai. (Apparently, Joshua did not go out to fight with the soldiers during the first battle between Israel and Ai.)

The Lord told Joshua that he and Israel would have a second chance to face Ai in battle. The Lord informed Joshua that Ai would suffer what Israel had suffered when there was sin in the camp—defeat.

Interestingly enough, although the Israelites were not permitted to keep the spoils in their victory against Jericho, this time God permitted them to take valuables (including livestock) and employ them for personal use. Had Achan waited on the Lord instead of disobeying the Lord's command regarding the valuables of Jericho, he would have been able to take valuables from Ai.

In the garden of Eden, Adam and Eve sinned against God. Eve saw, desired, and took the forbidden thing. Then they hid from the Lord. As believers, we face the choice of following God or disobeying Him. Every time we face sin and refuse to repent, we harden our hearts toward God. We run from Him and hide rather than run to Him and repent. The story of Achan reminds us of the terrible consequences of sin.

Achan had opportunities to repent. Each time he entered his tent, he knew of his stolen, hidden treasure. When Joshua instructed the people to consecrate themselves (Josh. 7:13), Achan should have repented during the process of consecration. Even before Joshua isolated Achan's family, Achan could have repented. Instead, because he hid his sin, Israel suffered a terrible defeat, and Achan lost everything—his life, his possessions, and his family. Sin resulted in death, and only after sin was dealt with could Israel move forward in victory.

When we harbor sin in our own lives, we are holding onto that which brings us death. Though the process of confessing sin might be painful and not without consequence, God's Word tells us that it's through confession of sin that we might find healing (Jas. 5:16). When we confess our sins, the community of faith around us has the opportunity to help us see the hope that Jesus brings. There is hope on the other side because Jesus has already taken on the penalty of our sin and now offers us freedom from sin in Himself.

After the sin in Israel was dealt with, God told Joshua not to be discouraged or afraid. What is the connection between hidden sin and discouragement or hidden sin and fear?

Are there any hidden sins in your life that must be confessed? With whom will you do so?

The Early Judges

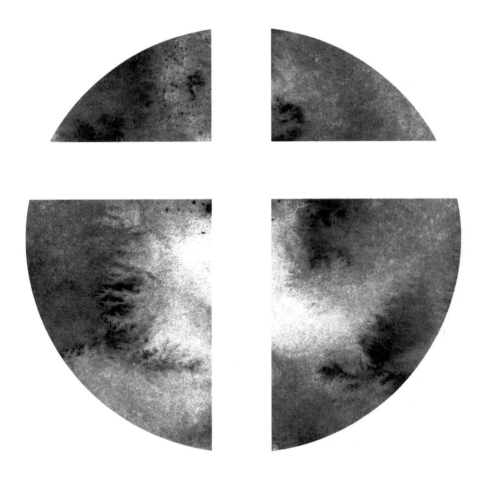

Introducing the Study

God is not only with His people; God is for His people. Whatever situation we might face in life, we can trust that God is not only with us but will actually fight for us. True enough, the victory He gives in these battles might not be the type of victory we anticipated, but our faith helps us continue to trust that the greatest victory for our souls has already been won in Christ.

 Why must we approach any battle we face with trust in both God's wisdom and power?

We often turn to God when the circumstances around us become desperate. And yet, when we perceive that everything is peaceful, we are tempted to lapse into spiritual laziness and complacency. If we are to live as the children of God, we must cultivate a lifestyle of dependence on and communion with God instead of only turning to Him as a last resort.

What are some ways we can live in a steady relationship with God instead of only turning to Him as a last resort?

Setting the Context

God's people were on the move. After their incredible victory at Jericho and their surprising defeat at Ai, the Lord continued to move His people further into **the promised land**. Each foe was defeated before Joshua and the army of Israel, and as they fell, God demonstrated over and over again that He is **the only true God**. These were more than battles over land; each victory for Israel was a victory for the Lord over the pagan gods of the Canaanites.

 With so many stories of God's faithfulness, why can it be difficult to trust that God is fighting for us?

As the conquest drew to a close, Joshua called on the people to **renew their covenant with the Lord**. The Israelites were about to settle in a land that had been filled with all kinds of idolatry and was still populated by people who worshiped false gods. The Lord knew that His people would be tempted to integrate the worship of idols into their spiritual lives. The people swore their allegiance, promising they would worship only the God of Israel, but their commitment to God and His covenant was short-lived.

It took only one generation before they began to worship foreign gods. Thus began the period of the judges, in which the Israelites fell into a pattern of sin, judgment, repentance, and deliverance, as shown in **"The Judges Cycle"** (p. 71). These stories remind us of our constant temptation to wander from the ways of God into sin.

Why do you think judgment and difficulties in life make us more prone to focus on spiritual things?

✝ CHRIST Connection

The judges saved people from the consequences of their sin but could not change the cause of their sin. Jesus is the Savior and Judge who takes upon Himself the consequences of our sin and then offers us new hearts that seek His righteousness.

The **Judges** Cycle

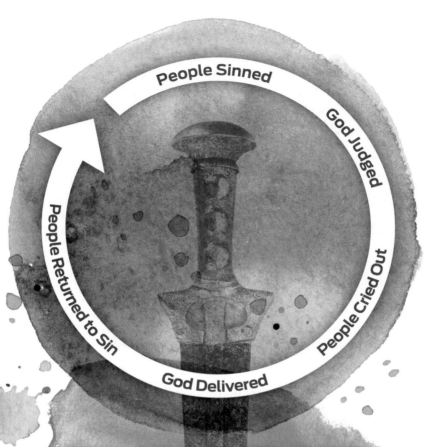

People Sinned

God Judged

People Cried Out

God Delivered

People Returned to Sin

God Raised Up Judges to Deliver the People

Othniel	Judges 3:7-11
Ehud	Judges 3:12-30
Deborah	Judges 4:1–5:31
Gideon	Judges 6:1–8:35
Jephthah	Judges 10:6–12:7
Samson	Judges 13:1–16:31

Continuing the Discussion

▶ Watch this session's video, and then continue the group discussion using the following guide.

What should we make of the repeated commands in Scripture to be strong, be courageous, and be holy?

What are some ways we can try to end the cycles of sin in our own lives? In our families? In our churches? In our communities?

As a group, read Judges 2:8-19.

✱ How could a generation rise up that did not know the Lord or what He had done?

What does that tell you about our responsibility for the next generation?

What do these verses reveal about our pull toward sin?

It only took one generation of neglect for the people to fall into this downward spiral of sin. The people would begin to worship other gods; then the Lord would judge their idolatry; then the people would call out for help, and the Lord would respond with a deliverer. But then the people would once again return to sin. The Book of Judges shines a harsh light on the human heart and our insistence upon our own way instead of God's.

As a group, read Judges 4:4-7.

What sticks out to you the most about this description of Deborah the judge?

✱ What must you believe to be true about God to take a courageous stand for Him?

Before God raised up Deborah as a judge, the people lived under the oppression of King Jabin and his commander Sisera for twenty years. Despite this long period of oppression, Deborah knew that the power of the Lord was stronger than the power of their enemies, and that knowledge gave her the boldness to move forward.

As a group, read Judges 4:14-16.

> Have you ever felt like Barak, in need of encouragement from someone else to do a difficult thing? What happened?

✱ Why might God actually desire to place us in difficult situations?

> What effect can facing difficult situations have on our faith?

At the urging of Deborah, Barak confronted an army of superior size and strength, and the battle went as she had promised. The Lord is ultimately the One who decides victory and defeat, and the Lord gave the army over to the Israelites. It is a great misunderstanding for us to believe God will only give us ease and comfort in this life. In fact, He will at times position us in difficult situations both to grow our faith and bring His glory.

✚ MISSIONAL Application

Record in this space at least one way you will apply the truth of Scripture as one who has been forgiven and freed in Jesus from the destructive nature of sin.

Personal Study 1

God provides leaders to save His people from their cycle of sin.

Read Judges 2:8-19.

The Book of Judges presents a cycle of sin and salvation that becomes a pattern for God's people. As Moses' successor, Joshua led Israel to great victories, but when Joshua and his generation died, "another generation rose up who did not know the LORD or the works he had done for Israel" (Judg. 2:10). The spiritual state of Israel, after the death of Joshua, is sad to see. Abandoning God led to embracing idols.

What led to such a quick descent from the faithfulness of Joshua to the faithlessness of the next generation? The young people "did not know the LORD" or what God had done for them. They failed to remember God and His glorious rescue of their ancestors. Amnesia produces apostasy!

So what would God do in response to His people abandoning Him? Well, we know that God keeps His promises, and one of the promises He made was to discipline them if they persisted in disobedience (see Lev. 26:17; Deut. 28:15). The people wanted to be like the surrounding nations, so God gave them what they wanted and delivered the Israelites into the oppressive hands of those very nations.

But as we've come to expect from previous stories about an incredibly gracious God, judgment wasn't God's last word to His people. As the author of Judges continued to summarize this tumultuous time in the history of Israel, he showed that after God's discipline came God's salvation.

When you put Judges 2:14 and 16 together side by side, you may find yourself scratching your head. God handed His people over to the enemy, and then He saved them from the enemy? How does that work? The answer, of course, is that God is both just and gracious at the same time. He "will not leave the guilty unpunished," He told Moses, and He is also "slow to anger and abounding in faithful love" (Ex. 34:6-7). God saved His people from their enemies because He was moved by their misery and groaning. These groans weren't necessarily cries of repentance. The word translated "groaned" (Judg. 2:18) is used two other times in the Old Testament of the Israelites, and in both cases, the word refers to Israel groaning under Egyptian slavery (Ex. 2:24; 6:5). Groaning, in this case, is what God hears and prompts Him to deliver His people in light of His covenant promises to Abraham.

God delivered His people from their enemies, not because His people fully turned their hearts away from idols and back to Him and not because they were truly repentant. He delivered them because of His great love. He was compassionate toward them in their misery, and so, He showed them undeserved kindness through the judges He raised up to rescue them.

The cycle of the judges continued after each moment of deliverance. As you see at the end of this passage, whenever the judges died, Israel returned to their sin and their downward spiral of corruption. What Israel needed wasn't a temporary deliverer but a Savior who would change their hearts. The good news for us is that in the person of Jesus Christ, God is both our great Judge and our great Savior. In Christ, we are set free from these continuing patterns of sin and destruction and set loose for God's mission in the world.

What are some ways we can fight against "spiritual amnesia"?

How can you help others see God's discipline in your life as an expression of fatherly love toward you?

How does kindness lead us to repentance?

Personal Study 2

God provides wisdom to trust and obey God.

Read Judges 4:4-7.

The Israelites began to live within a cycle of sin and rebellion, which would turn to repentance and rescue and then back to rebellion again. Unbelief was the root of the Israelites' idolatry. They did not believe that God could satisfy them. So they kept chasing after other gods by doing what was "evil in the sight of the LORD" (Judg. 4:1). In response, the Lord allowed them to be oppressed by a foreign king named Jabin through his general named Sisera. His army included nine hundred chariots—the tanks of warfare in that day—ready to terrify any enemy that would rise up. Finally, after twenty years, the people cried out to God.

Against the backdrop of the Israelites' unbelief stood a few individuals who were willing to serve God and use their gifts for His glory. This passage introduces us to Deborah and Barak, servants of the Lord who operated out of a deep understanding of who God is. They trusted in His word. Deborah and Barak employed their gifts for the Lord, and then they watched Him do something miraculous.

Once again, God gave His people an unlikely leader. He raised up Deborah to be the judge over God's people. Of the twelve judges in the book, Deborah was the only woman. She proclaimed God's word and faithfully spoke on His behalf. The people brought problems for her to consider and offer a judgment. She was a prophetess, and she was the only judge we see using her gift of wisdom while not leading the military.

Barak was Deborah's general, and he led the army of God's people. At first glance, it might seem like Deborah was filled with faith and Barak with fear, but this was probably not the case. Barak said he would fight Sisera's army—if Deborah would go with him. Deborah was the representative of God's voice in this passage. Barak wanted to know that God would be with him, just as Moses did in Exodus 33 when he begged God to be with the people of Israel.

At the same time, Barak knew that Deborah was filled with wisdom, which is likely why he was willing to listen to her. Through her counsel, Deborah demonstrated that the greatest end of wisdom is to trust and obey God. That's exactly the kind of wisdom that Barak needed. Barak demonstrated faith (Heb. 11:32), albeit hesitantly, and he obeyed by preparing an army of ten thousand men. Barak used the gifts God gave him to walk in faithfulness to his calling.

Here were two very different people—a female judge and a hesitant general—coming together to walk in faithfulness.

In this microcosm we see how the church today moves forward in unity, as one body with many parts. Some, like Deborah, lead with wisdom and counsel. Others volunteer to lead small groups and teach children. Some will change diapers in the nursery, while others will open their homes to foster children. All of us have a role to play in the body of Christ. As the apostle Paul would later write: "Now as we have many parts in one body, and all the parts do not have the same function, in the same way we who are many are one body in Christ and individually members of one another" (Rom. 12:4-5).

When we walk in faith by using our gifts, we realize we are not the center of the story. We no longer pretend that we are worthy of glory, which frees us to truly serve God and others. We are not the point of the story, but we point to the One who is.

What are some ways we can discover the gifts God has given us?

What happens when we choose not to use our gifts in service to God?

Personal Study 3

God provides courage to face impossible odds.

Read Judges 4:14-16.

As we continue the story, we see how God's chosen leaders used their gifts in the face of incredible odds. The day of war had arrived. The army of God was assembled on the top of Mount Tabor, and they could see the nine hundred chariots coming. You may think Sisera's opposing army was small compared to the Israelites' ten thousand men. But this was before the days of air war and automatic weapons. No one had ever seen an army of nine hundred chariots. Barak and his foot soldiers would not be able to overpower Sisera and his mobile force filled with men equipped for battle. Without divine help, Israel had no shot at victory.

Consider Barak's army: They knew they were out-gunned when it came to weapons (Judg. 5:8). The odds were stacked against them—except God was on their side. And so they stood there and wondered what God was going to do. Maybe they retold one another the story of the exodus: "Remember what God did when He parted the Red Sea and our fathers walked through on dry ground? Remember when our families came into the promised land with Joshua and the river was parted? What is He going to do now?"

Deborah, Barak, and the people of God had faith in the Lord's words. He said they would be victorious. Because He is a faithful God, their faith in His victory was secure.

The hinge of this narrative hangs on Judges 4:14: "Hasn't the LORD gone before you?" This was the place of confidence and hope for the people of God—the Lord had gone before them. There was nothing to fear because the Lord had prepared the way. Victory would be theirs because the Lord's promise was sure. The Lord, whom they had previously forsaken and abandoned, had not abandoned them.

Sometimes we make the mistake of thinking that if we are walking in the will of God, He will not lead us into danger, difficulty, or even seeming disaster, but nothing could be further from the truth. Jesus Himself promised His followers that they would have trouble (John 16:33). Being a Christian does not exempt us from the same struggles that come upon every other human being. In fact, being a Christian sometimes means that God intentionally leads us into difficult circumstances. Why might He do this?

First of all, God might lead us into such situations of seeming impossible odds for the sake of our faith. James tells us that it's through the testing of our faith that we develop perseverance and that we need perseverance in order to become mature and complete in Christ (Jas. 1:2-4). God's highest goal for His children is not ease, comfort, or stability but instead to be conformed to the image of Jesus. Difficulty is one of the ways He brings this about.

But God also might lead us into situations with overwhelming odds so that He will gain glory. If we look back at this story, we see that there is no good reason why Deborah and Barak would have been successful. The odds were stacked against them. When the deliverance came, there was no other option than for everyone to give God the glory in victory.

Faith in God is what leads us to be courageous when facing impossible odds. Faith is demonstrated by our belief and obedience, our trusting in God and desire to obey Him in faith. Our faith is not rooted in our gifting, found in our skills, or propped up by our ambitions. Our faith is in the sure Word of God and in His unshakable character. As the people of God, we build our lives on the promises of God. No other foundation is stable.

What is the significance of Deborah telling Barak that the Lord had gone out before him (Judg. 4:14)?

What happens when we have more faith in our gifts than in God's power?

The Later Judges

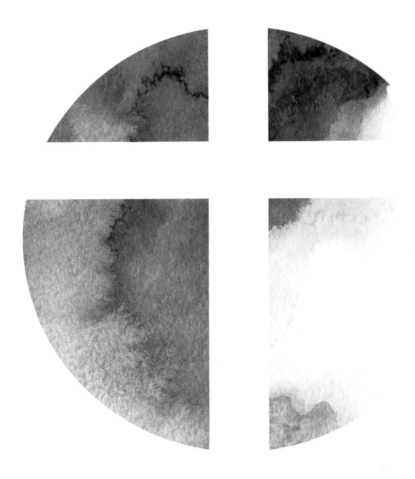

Introducing the Study

It has been said that sin will take you farther than you want to go, keep you longer than you want to stay, and cost you more than you want to pay. That's because sin is a downward spiral into greater and greater depths of disobedience, as we see with Israel in the Book of Judges. When we are caught in a cycle of sin like this, it often takes desperate measures to get our attention to call out to God.

> **In what ways have you seen this downward spiral of sin at play in the world around you?**

When we finally do cry out to God, He sometimes, in His mercy, provides some kind of relief for our circumstances. But God is interested in much more than making our circumstances better. He ultimately wants us to come to the realization that we are powerless to change our sinful hearts and that our greatest need is not circumstantial but eternal.

 How should knowing that God is most interested in providing for your eternal needs change the way you view your present circumstances?

Setting the Context

Once in the promised land, the Israelites soon adopted the pagan practices and idols of the people dwelling there. God would bring **discipline** on His people through oppression from the surrounding peoples, and then they would cry out to Him. In His mercy, God would raise up a deliverer—**a judge**—whom He would give amazing insight or abilities for the sake of the deliverance of His people.

> How have others used their spiritual gifts from God to serve and encourage you for the benefit of your faith in Jesus?

God's judges started with **Othniel**, Caleb's youngest brother, who brought peace to the land for forty years. **Ehud** assassinated King Eglon by stabbing him with such force that the king's fat closed over the hilt of his sword. **Deborah**, whom we read about in the previous session, gave military counsel and a great victory was won.

Then came **Gideon**, a most unlikely leader whom God used to defeat the Midianites, as we will see in this session. **Jephthah** delivered the people but at the cost of his own daughter due to a foolish vow. And of course, **Samson** was blessed by God with mighty strength to liberate his oppressed people, but he serves as a lasting example of the ultimate failure of all these judges. **"Seeing Jesus in the Judges"** (p. 83) shows us that Jesus is the greater, perfect Judge who was still to come.

 How does the downward spiral of sin in the people and the judges point us to our need for Jesus?

✝ CHRIST Connection

The judges were imperfect people whom God used in unexpected ways to deliver His people and show that He is the source of salvation. Jesus was the perfect Rescuer who defeated sin and death in an unexpected way to show everyone that salvation belongs to God alone. God used Christ's death and resurrection to bring deliverance "once for all" for His people.

Seeing Jesus *in the* Judges

OLD TESTAMENT	NEW TESTAMENT
The Judges Saved the People While Still Alive (Judg. 2:18)	**Jesus** Saves His People Forever, Being Raised from the Dead (Rom. 8)
Gideon's Army of 300 God's Glory Through Weakness (Judg. 7:2)	**Preach Christ Crucified** God's Power and Wisdom (1 Cor. 1:24)
Samson's Death Vengeance upon His Idolatrous Enemies (Judg. 16:28)	**Jesus' Death** Salvation for His Enemies Who Believe (Rom. 5:8-10)
Samuel A Prophet to Whom God Revealed Himself by His Word (1 Sam. 3:21)	**Jesus** In These Last Days, God Has Spoken to Us by His Son (Heb. 1:2)

Continuing the Discussion

 Watch this session's video, and then continue the group discussion using the following guide.

How do the judges show us that we need the perfect Judge in Jesus?

How should the absence of a king in Israel during the period of the judges prepare us to look forward to God's promised King?

As a group, read Judges 6:11-16.

What is strange about the way the angel addressed Gideon?

 What other biblical accounts does this conversation between the angel and Gideon remind you of?

Do you think there is a difference between how God sees you and how you see yourself? If so, what is it?

The angel's address to Gideon was strange given that he was hiding in a winepress from the oppressive Midianites. In the same way that Moses at first balked at God's call on him, so also did Gideon doubt that he could do what God was commanding. We too might look at our strength, talent, or circumstances and wonder whether God could use us. But despite how we see ourselves, God has an eternal view in mind, calling us sons and daughters even when we don't feel like it.

As a group, read Judges 7:15-22.

What does this victory demonstrate about the way God chooses to do His work?

What might God be calling you to do that doesn't make sense from an earthly standpoint?

Prior to these verses, God had whittled down Gideon's army to a fraction of its previous size. Based on size alone, the army of Israel would be no match for Midian. But God was positioning Gideon and the army to demonstrate that the battle truly belonged to Him.

As a group, read Judges 16:21-22,26-30.

How do these passages compare with the vision of Samson as a super-strong warrior for God?

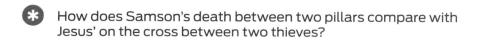 How does Samson's death between two pillars compare with Jesus' on the cross between two thieves?

Why do you think God chose to empower Samson at this moment, in spite of his faithlessness and disobedience?

Samson's story is tragic. Though gifted by God, he lived a life of pride, unwilling to acknowledge the source of his strength. And yet, at his moment of greatest need, he called out to God and received help and power, showing us that it's never too late to turn to the Lord.

✛ MISSIONAL Application

Record in this space at least one way you will apply the truth of Scripture as a faithful servant empowered by God to proclaim Jesus, our faithful Savior and Judge.

Personal Study 1

God provides strength to the weak.

Read Judges 6:11-16.

As we continue our journey through the storyline of Scripture, we see how the cycle of sin, oppression, and deliverance in Judges continued. In Judges 6, the Lord gave the people over to their enemies for a period of seven years. The situation was dire. God's people were forced to hide out in their own land, in dens they made for themselves in the mountains. Meanwhile, their enemies, the Midianites, overran their land, devoured their produce, and took their livestock. To deliver them, God raised up an unlikely man and chose to make a mighty warrior out of him.

When "the angel of the LORD" came to Gideon, he said, "The LORD is with you, valiant warrior," assuring Gideon of God's presence. Surprisingly, Gideon responded by questioning that fact based on their oppression by Midian. Like Gideon, we sometimes fail to see our sin and our guilt, and so, we rush to blame God for whatever we are going through. Sometimes our difficult circumstances are brought about by our own sinfulness but never because God has been unfaithful.

Next, Gideon protested against God's commission on the basis of his inadequacy, being the youngest in his family. Again, God's response—"I will be with you"—was a reminder that the power of deliverance was not in Gideon but in God's presence. God often assures His people by pointing them to His presence (Gen. 28:15; 46:4; Isa. 41:10). His company has always been our source of strength in the midst of the storms of life. That's why we say with the psalmist: "Even when I go through the darkest valley, I fear no danger, for you are with me" (Ps. 23:4).

"But I will be with you." Everything Gideon needed was supplied in that brief statement. Basically, God has nothing else or more to offer you. You can go through anything with that promise. It does not answer your questions about details; it only provides the essentials. "I will be with you"—and that is enough.

As followers of Christ, we trust in Jesus' promise to empower us through His Spirit (Acts 1:8). No matter how inadequate we may feel, God sees us and says, "Valiant warriors!" The strength to obey God and join Him on mission does not come from within us but from God's empowering Spirit. It's no wonder that the Great Commission ends with the same promise: "Go, therefore, and make disciples of all nations … I am with you always" (Matt. 28:19-20).

On the surface, it seems strange that Gideon responded with such terror to being in God's presence. Don't we want to sense God close to us? Don't we yearn for His presence in our lives? Perhaps the strangeness of Gideon's reaction is a sign that we have forgotten what an incredible gift it is to have access to God's power and presence.

In the days of the tabernacle and the temple in the Old Testament, only the high priest could go once a year behind the veil that separated the holy of holies (God's presence) from the people of God. When Jesus was crucified, this veil was torn in two. And after His ascension, Jesus sent the Holy Spirit to empower us and give us His presence forever. Maybe we need more of Gideon's awe at the presence of God so we can be truly grateful for God's presence and power and be stirred up to worship God for who He is.

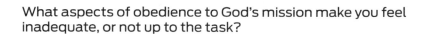

What aspects of obedience to God's mission make you feel inadequate, or not up to the task?

What aspects of God's presence might startle us?

What aspects of God's presence comfort and embolden us?

Personal Study 2

God provides victory to the obedient.

Read Judges 7:15-22.

The victory of Israel over Midian is one of the most extraordinary battle accounts in the Old Testament. God's power is made perfect in weakness (2 Cor. 12:9). And Gideon repeatedly demonstrated weakness: his lack of status and relative obscurity (Judg. 6:15), his fear of the Midianites in threshing wheat in a winepress (6:11), his fear of family and townspeople (6:27), his need for additional assurance (6:36-40), the radical reduction of his army (7:1-8), and his fear of the battle and need for additional encouragement (7:10-15).

Gideon was not a Hollywood hero; rather, his human weakness is highlighted throughout this story. Why? We see the answer in Judges 7:2, when God called for the reduction of Gideon's army: "or else Israel might elevate themselves over me and say, 'My own strength saved me.'" This is the key to salvation and to God's power. It is not in our effort but in our surrender. It's not about our impressive skills but about God's glory in salvation.

In Judges 7:1-8, God pared down the army from thirty-two thousand men to three hundred. God insisted that His people see their cause as utterly hopeless so that they would recognize that their deliverance could only be chalked up to God's power and mercy. Along the way, God continued to reassure Gideon. And finally, Gideon worshiped God as a sign of his faith that God would indeed accomplish His will through him.

God accomplished a unique and grand victory solely through His strength and wisdom. Even the manner of victory showed the battle belonged to the Lord and He had accomplished the victory. The three hundred men did not even attack; they pursued *after* the Midianites were fleeing.

Don't miss the picture of God granting victory through human weakness, as long as those human beings are depending on Him. We are saved in weakness and are being saved and sustained in weakness as we rely on Him. For example:

- **Sin:** We don't defeat sin simply by trying harder but by relying on God's Spirit and God's church.

- **Evangelism:** We don't win someone to Christ by intellect or by persuasive words but by relying on God to speak through us.

In our struggle against the enemy, we recognize that God displays His power through our weakness. We win the war from the inside out, by turning our hearts to Christ in faith.

The mind-set of our world is that great things are accomplished by strong people. How does the story of Gideon turn that mind-set upside down?

How does Gideon's story give you hope in your weakness?

Personal Study 3

God provides power to the desperate.

Read Judges 16:21-22, 26-30.

Samson's story is a classic tragedy. He was prideful, arrogant, and self-reliant, ironic considering that his great strength only came from God. Ultimately, his pride caught up with him and he was taken prisoner, humiliated by the same Philistines he had once conquered so easily. But as his life came to an end, Samson experienced true faith and repentance. He stopped trusting in his own strength and put his hope in God. This is the only time in Samson's life we see him praying.

Samson had run after sexual conquests, walked in violence and vengeance, disobeyed his parents, and did everything he knew to be wrong. But here he was a different man. Samson was at the end of himself. The Philistines captured him, plucked out his eyes, and turned him into a slave that ground grain. Oh, how the mighty have fallen!

Have you ever come to the end of your rope? Have you ever become desperate enough to turn to God and renounce reliance on anything else and surrender to Him? Has your battle with sin gotten the better of you so many times that you have nothing left to offer? This was the end of Samson's rope. He couldn't run any further from God. In the same way that God handed the Israelites over to their enemies for reproof and correction, God had handed over this judge of Israel. And this was the moment Samson found true strength—in his weakness.

At the end of his life, Samson cried out to God for enough strength to defeat the enemies of God's people who were present. God reached down into the brokenness of the judge who was chosen before his birth, and for the good of His people, He answered Samson's prayer. He rescued His people despite their total unbelief. Samson's downfall was the result of his own disobedience, and yet, God used his death to begin the deliverance of His people.

You might wonder if Samson actually believed in the Lord. If this were the only account of Samson we had in the Bible, we might have reason to wonder. But guess who shows up in Hebrews 11, the "Hall of Faith"? Samson (Heb. 11:32). Along with Abraham, Sarah, Isaac, Jacob, Moses, and David, we find the name of Samson, who walked by faith in God. Though it took Samson years for God to strip him of his pride, eventually this giant of a man was clothed in God's mercy.

Centuries later, another baby would come after the announcement of an angel. The angel told a young girl named Mary that she would carry the Deliverer of God's people in her womb and she should call the boy Jesus. This time the Deliverer would not need deliverance but would bring deliverance to the whole world. Jesus' death was the result of both His perfect obedience and our disobedience. And God used His death to bring deliverance "once for all" for His people.

Jesus is greater than Samson. He is the Judge who never breaks His word, the Judge who never operates out of impulse or for self-gratification. He only does the works of the Father, and by faith in His death and resurrection, many—including us—become sons and daughters of God.

In the story of Samson, God says to Christians: "I love you. I am your rescue. The gifts I've given you I gave because I'm a good Father. So when you look at your gifts and your personality and the blessings in your life, let worship run its full course back to Me." Let's not dare trust in ourselves.

It took humiliation and weakness to finally get Samson's attention. What are some circumstances God can use to get our attention and draw us back to Him?

What hope does it give us to see Samson mentioned as a man of faith in Hebrews 11?

Tips for Leading a Small Group

Follow these guidelines to prepare for each group session.

Prayerfully Prepare

Review
Review the weekly material and group questions ahead of time.

Pray
Be intentional about praying for each person in the group. Ask the Holy Spirit to work through you and the group discussion as you point to Jesus each week through God's Word.

Minimize Distractions

Create a comfortable environment. If group members are uncomfortable, they'll be distracted and therefore not engaged in the group experience. Plan ahead by considering these details:

Seating

Temperature

Lighting

Food or Drink

Surrounding Noise

General Cleanliness

At best, thoughtfulness and hospitality show guests and group members they're welcome and valued in whatever environment you choose to gather. At worst, people may never notice your effort, but they're also not distracted. Do everything in your ability to help people focus on what's most important: connecting with God, with the Bible, and with one another.

Include Others

Your goal is to foster a community in which people are welcome just as they are but encouraged to grow spiritually. Always be aware of opportunities to include any people who visit the group and to invite new people to join your group. An inexpensive way to make first-time guests feel welcome or to invite someone to get involved is to give them their own copies of this Bible study book.

Encourage Discussion

A good small-group experience has the following characteristics.

Everyone Participates
Encourage everyone to ask questions, share responses, or read aloud.

No One Dominates—Not Even the Leader
Be sure that your time speaking as a leader takes up less than half of your time together as a group. Politely guide discussion if anyone dominates.

Nobody Is Rushed Through Questions
Don't feel that a moment of silence is a bad thing. People often need time to think about their responses to questions they've just heard or to gain courage to share what God is stirring in their hearts.

Input Is Affirmed and Followed Up
Make sure you point out something true or helpful in a response. Don't just move on. Build community with follow-up questions, asking how other people have experienced similar things or how a truth has shaped their understanding of God and the Scripture you're studying. People are less likely to speak up if they fear that you don't actually want to hear their answers or that you're looking for only a certain answer.

God and His Word Are Central
Opinions and experiences can be helpful, but God has given us the truth. Trust God's Word to be the authority and God's Spirit to work in people's lives. You can't change anyone, but God can. Continually point people to the Word and to active steps of faith.

How to Use the Leader Guide

Prepare to Lead

Each session of the Leader Guide is designed to be **torn out** so you, the leader, can have this front-and-back page with you as you lead your group through the session.

Watch the session teaching video and **read through the session content** with the Leader Guide tear-out in hand and notice how it supplements each section of the study.

Use the **Session Objective** in the Leader Guide to help focus your preparation and leadership in the group session.

Questions and Answers

✱ Questions in the session content with **this icon** have some sample answers provided in the Leader Guide, if needed, to help you jump-start the conversation or steer the conversation.

Setting the Context

This section of the session always has an **infographic** on the opposite page. The Leader Guide provides an activity to help your group members interact with the content communicated through the infographic.

MISSIONAL Application

The Leader Guide provides a **MISSIONAL Application statement** about how Christians should respond to the truth of God's Word. Read this statement to the group and then direct them to record in the blank space provided in their book at least one way they will respond on a personal level, remembering that all of Scripture points to the gospel of Jesus Christ.

Pray

Conclude each group session with a prayer. **A brief sample prayer** is provided at the end of each Leader Guide tear-out.

Session 1 · Leader Guide

Session Objective

Show that God was at work to deliver His people from slavery in Egypt and return them to the land of promise He had given them through Abraham. (This session will take them to the brink of deliverance, so it will feel like part 1 of 2 in some ways.)

Setting the Context

Use these answers as needed for the questions highlighted in this section.

- A person under the slavery of sin is oppressed and burdened.
- The power to become free from slavery must come from outside oneself.
- Barring freedom and redemption, slavery holds sway over someone until death.

- God's faithfulness in the past proves His commitment to remain faithful in the future.
- Salvation from sin through repentance and faith in Jesus means He will one day fully and completely save us from the effects of sin.
- God's faithfulness despite all odds shows that He is in control and will accomplish our deliverance.

Use the following activity to help group members see how Moses' example means we are also able to be used by God in His mission.

Encourage group members to read over **"Moses' Life"** (p. 11).

- Ask: "Looking at the first eighty years of Moses' life, what difficulties would you expect him to have as a leader in God's plan?" *(Moses was spared from the oppression of his people for forty years as Pharaoh's grandson. Moses murdered an Egyptian taskmaster and then fled away from his people in fear. Moses lived in Midian away from the oppression of his people for another forty years. Moses had a foreign wife.)*

- Ask: "If God could overcome all of these obstacles in Moses' life, why do we continue to have excuses that God can't or shouldn't use us?" *(Because we struggle to believe in the grace and power of God. We often succumb to the shame and fear of our own sins. We believe there are limits to God's faithfulness.)*

Read this paragraph to transition to the next part of the study.

Regardless of our excuses, God is the great "I AM"; He is everything we need to live as holy and obedient children. We know this because of how He used Moses, but even more so because He has given us Jesus to rescue us from our slavery to sin.

Continuing the Discussion

Watch this session's video, and then as part of the group discussion, use these answers as needed for the questions highlighted in this section.

Exodus 3:2-10

- God is gracious and sovereign to use whom He wills.
- Though God appears to delay, He is faithful to fulfill His promises.
- God always hears the cries of His people.

Exodus 3:11-15

- God's presence with me matters more than my ability, or the lack thereof.
- The goal of obedience to God is worship to His great name, not to mine.
- God is everything we need for strength and obedience to do what He has called us to do.

Exodus 7:14-18

- God is in control over His creation.
- God's people would have seen that their oppressors were not as strong as they perceived them to be.
- The Egyptians would have been confronted with the weakness of their so-called gods and religious system.

Share the following statement with the group. Then direct them to record in the space provided in their book at least one way they will apply the truth of Scripture as a believer in the sovereign God who hears His people.

✝ MISSIONAL Application

Because God has delivered us from the oppression of sin through Christ, we strive to be conscious of the plight of the oppressed in our world as we seek justice for all and to show and share the love of God.

Close your group in prayer, thanking God for His ongoing presence in our lives and confessing His greatness over every false god.

Session 2 · Leader Guide

Session Objective

Show God's final acts of deliverance from Egypt and how the Passover lamb is a type of Jesus, who would be given as the Lamb who takes away the sin of the world.

Introducing the Study

Use these answers as needed for the question highlighted in this section.

- We could easily misunderstand the gravity and severity of the plagues, given our propensity to view God through our own self-centered lens.
- The plagues served a good purpose of tearing down the idols of the Egyptians so they could see how dead they actually are.
- We need to recognize that God's glory is of utmost importance for our existence and salvation.

Setting the Context

Use these answers as needed for the question highlighted in this section.

- God conquers our wayward hearts with His love and grace displayed to us in Jesus on the cross.
- Our salvation from sin is not something we can accomplish on our own but must come from God.
- Because we have been saved, we praise and proclaim Jesus as our Lord and Savior.

Use the following activity to help group members see the significance of a Christ-centered reading of Scripture.

Instruct group members to review the connections on **"Seeing Jesus in the Exodus"** (p. 23). Then ask the following questions: "Which connection stands out to you the most? Why?" "What do you make of the wide array of connections between the Old Testament and the New Testament: Jesus with God, a human being, a nation of people, and a sacrificial animal?"

Remind your group that the Bible is telling God's story of His creation and work in the world, and that story centers upon Jesus Christ. From the beginning and here, through the exodus, God was working to prepare people's hearts and minds to see and recognize Jesus for who He is—the promised Son of God sent to save His people from their sin, and all who come to Christ in faith are included as part of His people.

Continuing the Discussion

Watch this session's video, and then as part of the group discussion, use these answers as needed for the questions highlighted in this section.

Exodus 12:3-8,12-13

- Our good works compared to our bad works.
- The faith of our parents.
- Our baptism and church attendance.

Exodus 12:29-32

- Sin is a matter of life and death.
- These verses echo God's warning in the garden that the wages of sin is death.
- No one can escape the judgment of God against sin without falling upon His grace and mercy.

Exodus 14:13-28

- We have experienced the grace of God in our salvation from sin, yet we can be timid and fearful to share the gospel with others.
- We have felt the power of God when we have turned away from temptation, yet we still find ourselves struggling with temptation and sin.
- We've seen unlikely transformation in ourselves and our brothers and sisters in Christ, but we can still despair that a loved one seems beyond God's reach.

Share the following statement with the group. Then direct them to record in the space provided in their book at least one way they will apply the truth of Scripture as a witness to the power and sovereignty of the one true God over all His enemies and false idols.

MISSIONAL Application

God has spared us from judgment and freed us from sin through His Son, so we warn others of the coming judgment and offer the good news of salvation through Jesus, the substitute Lamb, to everyone around us.

Close your group in prayer, praising God for how He has delivered us in Christ and will keep us eternally safe in Him.

Session 3 · Leader Guide

Session Objective

Show how God was developing a relationship with His people as they traveled from Egypt toward the promised land, starting with instructions for how they could properly worship Him through obedience and sacrifices.

Introducing the Study

Use these answers as needed for the question highlighted in this section.

- God's desire for relationship with His people helps to keep His justice and judgment in perspective.
- This communicates God's heart to redeem and save His wayward people, not just write them off.
- We can know that God is close to us in our worship, in our struggles, and in our pain.

Setting the Context

Use these answers as needed for the question highlighted in this section.

- While the limits are different for every person, we all struggle to keep even human laws perfectly, and God's laws require perfection.
- Laws, being told to do or not do something, often surfaces a sinful desire to reject such instruction, which shows just how deep our sin problem goes.
- The problem with laws is they cannot change the heart, which is the root of our sin problem. Only the gospel of Jesus can change the heart.

Use the following activity to help group members see how Eden, the tabernacle, and Jesus all connect with one another.

Allow group members a moment to review **"The Tabernacle"** (p. 35). Then ask the following questions: "If you were to build a structure for God's presence, would you build an elaborate tent? Why or why not?" "Why do you think the tabernacle mirrors the garden of Eden?" "How does the Scripture that says Jesus 'dwelt,' or 'tabernacled,' among us (John 1:14) affect your perception of this tent?"

Explain that God's presence with His people and the revelation of His glory have been the heart of God since the beginning of His creation. Sin separates God's image bearers from the One they are to reflect, but in the tabernacle, and supremely in Jesus, God has taken steps to overcome His people's sin and to dwell with them once more.

Continuing the Discussion

Watch this session's video, and then as part of the group discussion, use these answers as needed for the questions highlighted in this section.

Exodus 20:1-8

- Love will naturally flow out in actions that display obedience.
- Obedience from the heart requires love, or else it is merely a self-centered action done for personal gain.
- Disobedience betrays a heart that struggles with love for God and others.

Exodus 20:12-17

- We demonstrate our love for God by obeying His commands, so relating rightly to others demonstrates our love for God.
- We love because He first loved us, so the source of our love for others comes from God Himself.
- Love for God will drive us to treat others kindly and to seek to make things right when we have wronged others.

Exodus 40:34-38

- The people knew God was with them every step of the way of their journey to the promised land.
- God visibly provided the people with direction and rest through His presence in the tabernacle.
- God provided light to the Israelites during nighttime through a fire in the cloud of His glory.

Share the following statement with the group. Then direct them to record in the space provided in their book at least one way they will apply the truth of Scripture as a tabernacle for the Spirit of God in this world.

MISSIONAL Application

Because Jesus has fulfilled the law in our place, we are now free to please God and display His redemptive purpose in our relationships with others.

Close your group in prayer, thanking God not only for showing us how to live but, through Jesus and the Holy Spirit, giving us the power to do so.

Session 4 · Leader Guide

Session Objective

Show that even though God had delivered His people and showed them how to have a relationship with Him, they turned from Him and rebelled repeatedly, echoing the ripples of sin we saw from the fall of humanity in the garden of Eden. Once again we see how hopeless our condition is because of our sin.

Introducing the Study

Use these answers as needed for the question highlighted in this section.

- Using the law to restore our relationship with God leads to pride and despair.
- As long as we see the perfection of the law as something attainable by us, we will never see our need for a Savior.
- Recognizing our inability to keep the law should drive us to humility before the God of the law, and God never turns away a humble heart (Ps. 51:17).

Setting the Context

Use these answers as needed for the question highlighted in this section.

- The law reveals God's expectation of perfect holiness, something only God Himself embodies, and He does so in Jesus Christ.
- Only Jesus can provide the law's perfect righteousness for us in our place.
- The law explains worship, sacrifices, and roles in the community, all of which point to Jesus Christ as the fulfillment of the law.

Use the following activity to help group members see God's purposes in the journey.

Ask group members to find the two roads from Egypt to Canaan on **"Journey to the Promised Land"** (p. 47). Say: "The quickest route between two points is a straight line, or in this case, a paved one, but quickest is not always best or right. God had purposes beyond ease in leading the people in the ways that He did." Then ask the following questions: "What did the people learn from the "dead end" path to the Red Sea?" "What might the people have learned by going out of the way to Mount Sinai?" "How should God's faithful, daily provision of food for the people have prepared them when they reached the edge of the promised land?"

God teaches His people through more than just instruction and law; He teaches them on the journey. The paths God leads us on prepare us for future paths, and the lessons we learn reveal who God is and who we are. We must learn from these lessons and learn from the mistakes of those who went before us (see 1 Cor. 10:1-13).

Continuing the Discussion

Watch this session's video, and then as part of the group discussion, use these answers as needed for the questions highlighted in this section.

Numbers 13:1-2,30-33

- Sin is the absence of faith or failing to act in faith.
  - "Without faith it is impossible to please God" (Heb. 11:6), which is the essence of sin.
  - Good works without faith are sinful at their core because they are not done for the glory of God.

Numbers 14:1-4,30-35

- The people believed God was deceitful and malicious.
  - The people believed God was weak and helpless against the peoples of Canaan.
  - The people believed God was unfaithful to His promises to Abraham, Isaac, and Jacob.

Numbers 21:4-9

- "The wages of sin is death" (Rom. 6:23).
  - Ultimate salvation requires that the serpent be crushed (Gen. 3:15).
  - Everyone who looks in faith to Jesus, who was lifted up on a cross, will not perish but have eternal life (John 3:16).

Share the following statement with the group. Then direct them to record in the space provided in their book at least one way they will apply the truth of Scripture as one who looks to Jesus in faith for salvation from sin and for eternal life.

MISSIONAL Application

Because we have been spared from punishment of sin through the intercession of Jesus, we plead with others to look upon the cross and receive salvation through Jesus Christ as well.

Close your group in prayer, asking God to help you and your group combat sin with faith in His good character and provision.

Session 5 · Leader Guide

Session Objective

Show how God brought about victory for His people in the land using the battles of Jericho and Ai as examples of the greater conquest and how Israel needed to trust God to fight for them.

Introducing the Study

Use these answers as needed for the question highlighted in this section.

- God doesn't provide according to my expected timetable.
- God's provision is not enough; I want more.
- God doesn't give me what I think I need.

Setting the Context

Use these answers as needed for the question highlighted in this section.

- A failure to pray constantly.
- Seeking revenge and taking matters into our own hands.
- Repeatedly falling into patterns of sin even though we as Christians have been freed from the slavery to sin.

Use the following activity to help group members see that God was with His people as they entered and conquered the promised land, just as He had said.

Ask group members to call out some significant details from the map **"Conquest of the Promised Land"** (p. 59), which might include clear ways the Lord was fighting for the Israelites, the overwhelming success of the Israelites in their battles even though they had been wandering in the wilderness for forty years, the lone defeat at Ai, and the breadth of area yet to be conquered in the promised land. Then ask the following question: "How does the success of these campaigns in the promised land relate to the fears of the previous generation of Israelites forty years earlier?

Read this paragraph to transition to the next part of the study.

Forty years earlier, the Israelites rejected the promised land for fear of its inhabitants rather than trust in the God who had liberated and cared for them. Then after recognizing their folly, they rejected the Lord's discipline and entered the promised land to conquer it but failed because the Lord was not with them. The Bible passages in this session deal with Joshua's central campaign, the victory over Jericho and the defeat then victory over Ai, and the fate of their battles depended upon the Lord's presence.

Continuing the Discussion

Watch this session's video, and then as part of the group discussion, use these answers as needed for the questions highlighted in this section.

Joshua 6:1-5

- God wanted to prove to the Israelites that He was going to fight for them.
- God wanted all the glory from the battle to go to Himself.
- God wanted the Israelites to retain a humble and obedient posture in their new land.

Joshua 7:1-12,24-26

- Sin has a wider range of consequences than we can imagine.
- Tolerating and condoning sin is disastrous, both for the sinner and the enabler.
- Secret sins are known to the Lord, and He will judge them.

Joshua 8:1-2

- Having dealt with the sin in the camp, the Lord spoke to the Israelites as before, with comfort and encouragement.
- The people had lost a battle, but they had not lost the war, and the Lord was still fighting for them.
- The Lord had the battle in hand and He would grant victory to the people if they would obey.

Share the following statement with the group. Then direct them to record in the space provided in their book at least one way they will apply the truth of Scripture as a strong and courageous believer in Jesus Christ, who fights His enemies on behalf of His people.

MISSIONAL Application

Because we have experienced victory over sin and death through Jesus, we tell people of every tribe and nation about Jesus so they too might trust in Him and become part of the one people of God.

Close your group in prayer, thanking God for His willingness to give the greatest victory of salvation to His children.

Session 6 · Leader Guide

Session Objective

Show how God's people continued in a tailspin of sin and rebellion against Him, yet in His mercy and kindness, He provided judges to rescue them. While these judges pointed the people back to God, they could not address their sin problem, which is why the cycle of sin continued.

Introducing the Study

Use these answers as needed for the question highlighted in this section.

- Our battles may seem beyond us, so we need to trust God's wisdom in allowing these circumstances into our lives.
- We need to fight our battles with God's power and God's weapons, otherwise we will succumb to pride or despair, depending upon the outcome.
- God's ways and thoughts are higher than our own, and He knows how we should prevail over all of our trials and battles.

Setting the Context

Use these answers as needed for the question highlighted in this section.

- Sin in our lives may be resulting in discipline and natural consequences.
- The enemies and circumstances of the moment can overwhelm our faith and take our eyes off of God.
- In our pride, we can be expecting a certain outcome that doesn't match up to what God has planned.

Use the following activity to help group members see the futility of freedom without addressing the heart of sin.

Instruct group members to look at **"The Judges Cycle"** (p. 71), and then call for six volunteers to read some brief passages from the Book of Judges. These passages detail the first three phases of the Judges cycle with the six main judges named at the bottom of the infographic. *(Encourage the volunteers not to stress about the names, just to give them a good try and move on.)*: • Judges 3:7-9a • Judges 3:12-15a • Judges 4:1-3 • Judges 6:1-6 • Judges 10:6-10 • Judges 13:1.

Ask: "What are your impressions of the Israelites after reading those passages back to back?" "What are some ways we might fall into a similar cycle?"

Conclude this activity by reading the "CHRIST Connection" (p. 70).

Continuing the Discussion

Watch this session's video, and then as part of the group discussion, use these answers as needed for the questions highlighted in this section.

Judges 2:8-19

- The Israelites did not pass on their stories of faith and God's faithfulness to their children.
- The Israelites failed to obey God's command to teach their children the ways of God.
- The next generation may have rejected what was taught to them by their parents, seeing a more enticing form of religion from their pagan neighbors.

Judges 4:4-7

- That God is all-powerful and He protects His people.
- That God keeps His promises, that no matter the consequences from a courageous stand for Him in this life, the eternal life to come will make all those consequences pale in comparison.
- That God exists and rewards those who seek Him (Heb. 11:6).

Judges 4:14-16

- Difficult situations challenge our faith and help to strengthen our faith in God.
- Difficult situations provide a unique opportunity for God to demonstrate His power and glory to and through His people.
- Those who would enjoy seeing or placing Christians in difficult situations can be shocked and convicted when the Lord comes through for His people.

Share the following statement with the group. Then direct them to record in the space provided in their book at least one way they will apply the truth of Scripture as one who has been forgiven and freed in Jesus from the destructive nature of sin.

✝ MISSIONAL Application

Because we have been forgiven of our rebellion through Christ, we identify and resist the prevailing idolatries in our society so that our distinctiveness will back up our proclamation of the gospel.

Close your group in prayer, praying that God will give you courage to live in holiness no matter what excuses you might want to make.

Session 7 · Leader Guide

Session Objective

Show that God provided what the judges lacked so that it would be clear that salvation is truly from God and show the inverse function of how the later judges looked like greater rescuers but in reality proved to be less able to deliver God's people, demonstrating the need for the perfect Judge who was to come.

Introducing the Study

Use these answers as needed for the question highlighted in this section.

- My present uncomfortable circumstances are temporary.
- God works all things together for the good of those who love Him (Rom. 8:28).
- I should set my mind on things above, not on earthly things (Col. 3:1-2).

Read this paragraph to transition to the next part of the study.

The Book of Judges presents a dichotomy for us as we read it. On the one hand, it contains some of the most exciting and interesting stories in the Bible. But on the other hand, the book reveals the downward spiral of sin the Israelites were caught in.

Setting the Context

Use these answers as needed for the question highlighted in this section.

- Apart from a change in the heart, the cycle of sin will continue downward into deeper and deeper judgment from God.
- No matter their skill sets or spiritual gifts, no human leader can change a heart.
- Ultimately, every human being, including yourself, will let you down; only Jesus can sustain you and hold you in His hand forever for salvation.

Use the following activity to help group members see that both the strength and the weakness of the judges points to Jesus as the greater Judge.

Encourage group members to review the Old Testament and New Testament connections on **"Seeing Jesus in the Judges"** (p. 83). Ask: "What do the statements about Gideon and Samson call to mind regarding stories told in popular culture?" "Why does human weakness reveal God's strength and glory?" "Why does human strength ultimately reveal human weakness?"

Emphasize the first point that the work of the judges lasted only as long as they were alive, like so much work done by people today. But Jesus' work on the cross lives with Him and for us because He was raised from the dead, having defeated sin and death.

Continuing the Discussion

Watch this session's video, and then as part of the group discussion, use these answers as needed for the questions highlighted in this section.

Judges 6:11-16

- Abraham questioned how God could provide him with a son when he and Sarah were so old.
- Moses wanted God to choose someone else as His spokesperson because he felt ill-equipped and afraid.
- Joshua questioned the plan of God when the Israelites were defeated at Ai, believing the Canaanites would rally together and destroy them.

Judges 7:15-22

- God works in such a way as to humble His people and bring Himself glory.
- God works through the obedience of His people, even when that obedience doesn't make sense given the circumstances.
- No enemy and no army can prevail over God's people when He fights for them.

Judges 16:21-22,26-30

- In his strength, Samson died with vengeance against his enemies on his mind; Jesus died calling for forgiveness for those who were crucifying Him.
- Samson's death was more effective than he had been in his life; Jesus' life and death combine together to save a multitude beyond number from their sins.
- Samson prayed for God to remember him; Jesus was asked by one of the thieves to remember him when He entered into His kingdom, which He did.

Share the following statement with the group. Then direct them to record in the space provided in their book at least one way they will apply the truth of Scripture as a faithful servant empowered by God to proclaim Jesus, our faithful Savior and Judge.

✚ MISSIONAL Application

Because we have been rescued from our sin through Jesus, we answer His call to service, trusting that He is with us and will empower us to win the victory for His glory.

Close your group in prayer, expressing your trust that God will shine through your weakness to make Himself and His kingdom known.

BUT NOW IN CHRIST JESUS,

you who were far away
have been brought near
by the blood of Christ.

EPHESIANS 2:13

FROM COVER
TO COVER,

the Bible is the story of God's plan to redeem sinners through Jesus—the gospel. Gospel Foundations tells that story.

Be sure to take advantage of the following resources if you're planning a churchwide study. Even the *Single Group Starter Pack* offers significant savings.

CHURCH LAUNCH KIT (DIGITAL)

Want to take your entire church through Gospel Foundations? You'll want a *Church Launch Kit*. It includes sermon outlines, promotional graphics, and a Wordsearch Bible digital library for all leaders valued at $330. The *Kit* comes complimentary with every *Church Starter Pack*. Also available separately.

$29.99

Order online, call 800.458.2772, or visit the LifeWay Christian Store serving you.

STARTER PACKS

You can save money and time by purchasing starter packs for your group or church. Every *Church Starter Pack* includes a digital *Church Launch Kit* and access to a digital version of the *Leader Kit* videos.

Single Group Starter Pack
(10 *Bible Study Books*, 1 *Leader Kit*)
$99.99

Church Starter Pack - Small
(50 *Bible Study Books*, 5 *Leader Kit* DVDs, *Church Launch Kit*)
$449.99

Church Starter Pack - Medium
(100 *Bible Study Books*, 10 *Leader Kit* DVDs, *Church Launch Kit*)
$799.99

Church Starter Pack - Large
(500 *Bible Study Books*, 50 *Leader Kit* DVDs, *Church Launch Kit*)
$3495.99

LifeWay.com/GospelFoundations

Prices and availability subject to change without notice.

GOSPEL FOUNDATIONS

Longing for a King

VOL. 3	1 SAMUEL – 1 KINGS

A Year Through the Storyline of Scripture   LifeWay.

Continue your study of the bigger story of Scripture.

———

This volume reveals that though God's people live in the promised land, they are not free. Their rebellion against their Redeemer has led to their oppression. They long for a king to overthrow their enemies and lead them into prosperity. In *Longing for a King*, groups will learn that God was faithful to His promise to provide kings to lead His people. But even the best of these human kings could not overthrow their greatest oppressor— the sinfulness of their hearts. (7 sessions)

Bible Study Book $9.99
Leader Kit $29.99

Group Directory

Name: _____

Home Phone: _____

Mobile Phone: _____

Email: _____

Social Media: _____

Name: _____

Home Phone: _____

Mobile Phone: _____

Email: _____

Social Media: _____

Name: _____

Home Phone: _____

Mobile Phone: _____

Email: _____

Social Media: _____

Name: _____

Home Phone: _____

Mobile Phone: _____

Email: _____

Social Media: _____

Name: _____

Home Phone: _____

Mobile Phone: _____

Email: _____

Social Media: _____

Name: _____

Home Phone: _____

Mobile Phone: _____

Email: _____

Social Media: _____

Name: _____

Home Phone: _____

Mobile Phone: _____

Email: _____

Social Media: _____

Name: _____

Home Phone: _____

Mobile Phone: _____

Email: _____

Social Media: _____

Name: _____

Home Phone: _____

Mobile Phone: _____

Email: _____

Social Media: _____

Name: _____

Home Phone: _____

Mobile Phone: _____

Email: _____

Social Media: _____

Name: _____

Home Phone: _____

Mobile Phone: _____

Email: _____

Social Media: _____

Name: _____

Home Phone: _____

Mobile Phone: _____

Email: _____

Social Media: _____